KNOWLEDGE AND POWER

IN MOROCCO

KNOWLEDGE AND POWER
IN MOROCCO

The Education
of a Twentieth-Century
Notable

DALE F. EICKELMAN

PRINCETON UNIVERSITY PRESS

PRINCETON, NEW JERSEY

Copyright © 1985 by Princeton University Press
Published by Princeton University Press, 41 William Street
Princeton, New Jersey 08540
In the United Kingdom: Princeton University Press
Oxford

All Rights Reserved

Library of Congress Cataloging in Publication Data will be
found on the last printed page of this book

ISBN 0-691-09415-2
ISBN 0-691-02555-X (pbk.)

Second printing, for the paperback edition, 1992

Publication of this book has been aided by a grant from the
Paul Mellon Fund of Princeton University Press

This book has been composed in Linotron Sabon

Princeton University Press books are printed on acid-free
paper, and meet the guidelines for permanence and durability
of the Committee on Production Guidelines for Book
Longevity of the Council on Library Resources

Printed in the United States of America

3   5   7   8   6   4   2

To
Amal and Miriam

CONTENTS

CONTENTS

ILLUSTRATIONS

TABLES

MAPS

FOREWORD

by Clifford Geertz

IT USED TO BE that people called ethnographers asked questions and people called informants answered the questions, which the ethnographers duly recorded and worked into monographs, but things don't work that way anymore. It is not merely that the subjects of ethnographical study are increasingly unwilling to submit to so one-sided an exchange, one which reduces them to walking-around archives from which data are to be extracted; ethnographers have a clearer understanding of what it is they must do if they are to comprehend people different from themselves—start a conversation and maintain one. It is dialogue that does it, however delicate and liable to misfire, not inquisition, however orderly and straight from the shoulder.

But if Notes and Queries anthropology is dead or dying, along with the "we are the knowers, you are the known" cultural confidence that generated it, it is not always possible to discern the fact from anthropological writings which are still most commonly presented as summary reports of distant discoveries: rocks from the moon. There have been some scattered attempts to make the dialogical nature of contemporary ethnographic research more apparent to the world at large, but they have largely consisted in informal prefaces, personal confessions, or word-literal reproductions of particular interchanges, all of which more evoke the fact than put it to analytical use. There have been only a very few studies in which the anthropological conversation has been used to reshape the way in which material is presented and its implications explored. It is to this select company that Dr. Eickelman's work belongs. Setting the relation between himself, an intrusive

American intellectual, and Qadi Hajj Abd ar-Rahman Mansuri, a rooted Moroccan one, at the very center of his narrative, he has altered the form of a scholarly genre.

He has also extended its reach. His attempt to write a "social biography"—an account of his struggle to describe a traditional Islamic educational system and that of a rural judge to make his way through that system, set against the background of their momentarily converging lives—makes it possible for Eickelman to approach some typical anthropological issues in a quite untypical way. It is not just local color that this "The Judge and I" approach to things provides (though it does that too), nor but a backstage view of how an ethnographer works (though such a view is usefully demystifying). It provides an unusual angle from which to view an old and powerful cultural institution—an angle rather close to that from which its champions, or its prisoners, themselves view it.

The sense of what description and explanation amount to in anthropology that emerges from Eickelman's pages is thus a quite distinctive one. It is not at all usual to find in a work such as this extended discussions of the pursuit of a cache of disintegrating manuscripts through a labyrinth of factional jealousy, proprietary claims, family secrecy, and cultural suspicion. Even less, does one expect to encounter images of a young fieldworker and an indigenous scholar, thirty years his senior, bent over such manuscripts, admiring calligraphy, hunting for traces of economic dependencies, reading between the lines of political gossip, and discoursing on caravans and dress codes. And, perhaps least of all, is it common to come upon vignette narratives of such an odd couple working together, like a good cop and a bad cop, to worm the true story of a tribal massacre out of a peasant intruder at a landlord luncheon. An Eickelman explicitly remarks, what we have here is not a Berber judge "speaking for himself" (something he does quite well in his own ways, with his own means, and to his own ends), nor an American anthropologist speaking for him (something he is in no position, morally or intellectually, to do). What we have is a mixture of these unlike and jostling voices inscribed in a text: a "social document" in which they can be heard happily discoursing.

It is out of this discoursing that the substantive contributions of Eickelman's study come. The very figure of the qadi, reflective, questioning, shrewd, and knowledgeable in everything from linguistics to jurisprudence, undercuts the "wild west" image of Morocco (horses, guns, and wild-eyed holy men), and the story of his career, mosque school to Muslim university, demolishes the notion (one not only foreigners share, but many "évolué" Moroccans as well) that Islamic education was decadent there at its birth and declined thereafter. A simple opposition of an oral tradition and a written one, the first mindless and habitual, the second self-conscious and critical, can hardly survive a man who *first* reduces texts to memory—the Quran, a rhymed grammar, a legal handbook—and *then* starts to employ Arabic as a spoken language. (I once asked a Moroccan oral poet how he acquired his skill. "I memorized the Quran," he said; "Then I forgot the sentences and remembered the words.") The picture of the qadi and his brother's constant movement back and forth between a Muslim Podunk like Bzu or Boujad and a Muslim Paris like Marrakesh similarly dissolves any very sharp distinction between "great" and "little" traditions, "normative" and "folk" Islam, or urban cosmopolitanism and rural provincialism. ʿAbd ar-Rahman escapes a lot of categories.

But it is not from his side only that enlightenment comes. Dr. Eickelman's role in the conversation is hardly passive; he is no I-am-a-recorder anthropologist registering what he sees and hears and passing it on uninterfered with. The formulation of "Islamic knowledge" in Morocco as a matter of "mnemonic possession," the connection of such a notion to the means by which such knowledge is developed and transmitted, and the observation that elsewhere in the Islamic world—Oman, Iran—other notions lead to other means define ʿAbd ar-Rahman's style of thought in a way he is unlikely to be able to do himself, or, indeed, concerned with more instant matters, to have much interest in doing.

So do the careful tracing of the interplay between scholastic and brotherhood currents within Moroccan Islam, of the origins and nature of "reformism" within it, of its vicissitudes in the nationalist period, and of its present state and possible futures. The intrusion of a Western perspective, cast in terms of "cultural capital," "the stranger" and "the art of memory," does not displace the Moroccan perspective, blot it out with alien conceptions—it reframes it. It makes of the Qadi's Story much more than a recounting of a life. It makes of it, in good Muslim fashion as a matter of fact, an emblem and figuration of the civilization in which it was formed.

PREFACE

THIS BOOK concerns the changing role of Islamic education, the concept of knowledge inherent in it, and the relation of its carriers to wider society from the early years of colonial rule in twentieth-century Morocco to the present. These complex themes are concretely presented through an intensive "social biography," an approach which allows them to be explored in contextual detail without losing sight of more general issues of historical and social thought.

The subject of this study is a rural judge whose life and self-description contribute significantly to understanding the changing social role of religious intellectuals. Biography is a time-honored genre in American anthropology, and there are distinguished antecedents for the anthropological study of traditional intellectuals. Yet only in recent years have these concerns begun to be linked explicitly to the main currents of anthropological thought.

"Traditional" religious education, which thrived in Morocco until the 1930s, carried with it a sense of career which profoundly influenced the self-image of its carriers and their perception by others. Although the institutions of higher learning described in this study continue today only in highly altered form, the pervasive notions of personal responsibility, economic activities, and political authority shaped by them remain influential. Since the Iranian revolution, studies of Islam have focussed upon "resurgent" and militant movements. This study suggests alternative, popularly supported Islamic attitudes toward the contemporary world that form part of the background against which more radical Islamic visions can be better understood. It is also intended to complement studies of Islamic education in earlier historical periods, which have mostly concentrated upon institutional development and the political role of urban men of learning.

At another level, this book seeks to challenge the conventional view in Islamic studies and in studies of the Third World in general that "traditional" intellectuals constitute a social category of declining significance in modern political and cultural life. Western scholars have for the most part downplayed the vitality of Islamic learning in the modern era, a neglect reinforced by the tendency of nationalists and technocrats in North Africa and elsewhere to deny significance to men of learning whose notions of political action have differed from their own. Throughout widely fluctuating national political contexts, the ideas of knowledge prevalent in traditional Islamic education have continued to be largely congruent with popular understandings of religious knowledge. More than the study of earlier "golden" eras, a critical analysis of Islamic learning and its carriers in twentieth-century Morocco suggests the intricate ways in which ideas of learning and their modes of transmission influence, and in turn are influenced by, the shifting historical and political contexts in which they are maintained and reproduced.

A number of people have generously contributed to shaping this book through extensive discussions, readings of earlier versions, and practical advice during my stays in Morocco. Early discussions with Ernest Gellner and the late Lloyd A. Fallers first suggested to me the range of issues related to the study of traditional intellectuals. Clifford Geertz provided intellectual support when this book began to take practical shape, especially during my tenure as a member of the Institute for Advanced Study, Princeton, during the 1976-1977 academic year. As editor, Margaret Case provided strategic encouragement throughout its writing. Şerif Mardin, who has been working on comparable issues in Turkey, has also generously shared his ideas with me, and has allowed me to quote in Chapter Seven from a work in progress. David Hart, an institution in his own right, has set a standard of collegiality in sharing his Moroccan experiences that his Moroccan and foreign successors can aspire to emulate, and Kenneth Brown provided useful suggestions regarding the life of Mukhtar as-Susi.

Muhammad Aafif of the Université Mohamed V (Rabat) is largely responsible for introducing me to recent historical writing in Arabic, has verified Arabic usage throughout the text, and in innumerable ways has helped me appreciate Morocco's contemporary intellectual traditions. Ross Dunn of San Diego State University and Lawrence Rosen of Princeton University have likewise offered valuable advice that has contributed to shaping the present text. Dr. Fred A. Levin, Assistant Professor of Clinical Psychiatry, Northwestern University School of Medicine, and Instructor, The Institute for Psychoanalysis (Chicago), has put his earlier training as an anthropologist to use in helping me explore the personal relationships depicted in this text. Abdellah Hammoudi and Roy P. Mottahedeh have also provided useful comments. Christine Eickelman's suggestions for this manuscript have as always been perceptive.

For the discussion of specific points and practical assistance in meeting participants in Morocco's traditional learning, I am especially grateful to Attouarti Ali ben Mouallem (Marrakesh), Hajj Ahmad bin 'Abd as-Salam al-Bu 'Ayyashi (Tangier), Mohammed Cherkaoui (Casablanca), Bouzekri Draiouiy (Casablanca), Miloudi Draiouiy (Boujad), and Najmi Mohammad (Casablanca). For nearly two decades, I have benefited from the intellectual encouragement and hospitality of friends and colleagues at Morocco's institutions of higher learning and have sought whenever possible to strengthen the practical ties between our institutions. If these colleagues are not mentioned by name, I nonetheless feel an equal gratitude toward them.

Finally, I thank Qadi Hajj 'Abd ar-Rahman Mansuri and his family. Hajj 'Abd ar-Rahman agrees with me that disguising their identity in a book of this nature would have obscured much of the specific networks of learning that this book is intended to explore. I hope that the final version of this book merits the trust they have placed in me. Final responsibility for errors of fact and for interpretation is mine alone. To Hajj 'Abd ar-Rahman is the credit for the openness and creativity characteristic to the world of traditional Islamic learning.

Portions of this book, especially Chapters Four and Five, appeared earlier in *Comparative Studies in Society and History* 20 (1978). The two maps have been prepared by Michael Bonine of the University of Arizona.

Arabic names and terms are fully transliterated upon first occurrence only and in the glossary. Any analysis which draws upon extensive interviews as well as written sources must necessarily cross the line between colloquial and written usage. I have usually given precedence to the colloquial form of terms and phrases.

KNOWLEDGE AND POWER

IN MOROCCO

INTRODUCTION

LEARNING AND THE STATE

The nineteenth century was a period of intellectual ferment for scholars and students at Morocco's mosque-universities. In spite of the growing involvement of European powers in Morocco from the 1830s onward and the steadily worsening financial situation of the Moroccan state, higher education thrived and was alive with attempts at reform. As early as the reign of Sultan Sīdī Muḥammad bin 'Abd ar-Raḥmān (r. 1859-1873), mathematics, engineering and astronomy were reintroduced as taught subjects, admittedly on a rudimentary level. Men of learning associated with the government were in the vanguard of the reform movement. At the center of reformist thought of the period was a rededication to the values which made the Islamic community (*umma*) great in the past. Through personal and collective effort (*ijtihād*) and a renewed discipline of self and society through education and control (*niẓām*), they considered that Islamic society would become revitalized, offset the growing European challenge, and at the same time accept useful contemporary innovations (Binsa'īd 1983: 28-33). To achieve this goal, some religious scholars were ordered to pursue studies, including military science, in Egypt and in Europe (al-Manūnī 1973: 96-103; 114-125). The introduction of a lithograph printing press in Fez by 1865 significantly accelerated the diffusion of knowledge (Ayache 1979: 147; al-Manuni 1973: 203-212).

Sultan Mūlāy Ḥasan I (r. 1873-1894) also strongly encouraged scholars imbued with modernist, reform-minded ideologies derived from studies in the Arab East, primarily Cairo and Mecca. He took a personal interest in the debates of men of learning ('*ulamā*'; s. '*ālim*) (Jirārī 1976: 17-18) and encouraged higher education. His concern for higher religious studies was integrally linked to his efforts, not always successful, to modernize and expand the *Makhzan* (lit. "storehouse" or "coffer"), the name by which Morocco's government continues to be known. These efforts necessarily involved recruiting men of learning for the administration. Likewise Mulay ʿAbd al-Ḥāfiẓ, who was deputy sultan (*khalīfa*) in Marrakesh prior to assuming rule himself (r. 1908-1912), was recognized as a scholar in his own right. Like some of his predecessors, he took a direct interest in propagating reformist Islam (Burke 1976: 135).

Despite occasional setbacks, reformist ideologies had become quite influential in Morocco's ruling circles and with urban notables by the early twentieth century (Burke 1976: 37, 101, 135). There was a direct link between state authority (*quwwa; sulṭa*) and progress (*al-taqaddum*). At crucial moments in precolonial Morocco, as elsewhere in the Islamic world at earlier periods, men of learning played significant, if not always willing, political roles as spokesmen for the community (Burke 1972; 1976: 114-117; cf. Bulliet 1972; Hourani 1968; Lapidus 1967; Mottahedeh 1980). At the same time, Morocco's rulers recognized the support of men of learning as a profound source of legitimacy (al-Fassi 1954: 276-277).

Until 1925, the convergence of popular and royal support for learning was exemplified in the annual feasts for religious students, discussed in Chapter Four, held at both the Qarawiyīn mosque-university (*jāmiʿa*) in Fez and the Yūsufiya in Marrakesh. Students at both institutions selected a "mock" sultan among their numbers and other students formed his entourage. These feasts culminated in a public parody of Makhzan ceremonial, including the sermons (*khuṭba*s) delivered on Fridays and feast days. Often the real sultan was in attendance enjoying the spectacle, and the "mock" sultan had the right at the end of his "reign" to ask a favor of the real sultan.

Public recognition of the special role played by religious studies—no other category of Moroccans were accorded license equivalent to that of the students of religion—continued after the advent of colonial rule. At least once, in 1915, Marshal Hubert Lyautey, Morocco's first Resident-General, personally attended the Feast of Students in Fez (Bidwell 1973: 19). Colonial authorities were acutely sensitive of the political overtones of the event and finally sought to curtail the practice in 1925 (Cénival 1925: 139). Nonetheless, the Feast of Students continued on a reduced scale until the early 1960s. Traditionally educated men of learning continued to enjoy widespread respect.

Morocco's two mosque-universities continued to attract children of the country's intellectual and political elite until the 1930s. At the Qarawiyin and the Yusufiya, men of learning acquired a culturally valued cognitive style, "a set of basic, deeply interiorized master-patterns" of language and thought on the basis of which other patterns are subsequently acquired (Bourdieu 1967: 343), as distinct in its own way as was the tradition of learning epitomized by the *leçon* in French higher education. In spite of the effective collapse of traditional Is-

FIGURE 1. The Sultan of Tulba, Fez, 1925. [Reprinted with permission from *Hespéris* 5 (1925)].

lamic higher education in the 1930s, the cognitive style exemplified by men of learning continued to be the most popularly respected form of knowledge, shaping the language of politics and political action.

The disjunction between the collapse of higher Islamic education in the 1930s and the continued respect for the culturally valued knowledge which these institutions transmitted and reproduced provides a useful point of departure for exploring the relation between systems of meaning and the social contexts in which they occur. There is an anthropological tradition, still very much alive, that presumes a direct, one-to-one correlation between ideology and social action (e.g., Douglas 1973; Durkheim 1915; Evans-Pritchard 1940; Lienhardt 1967; Mauss 1966). However questionable such an assumption of correspondence may be when applied to "simple" societies, it is decidedly inadequate when applied to societies such as Morocco that are complex, internally differentiated, and historically known. As Emile Durkheim recognizes in his largely neglected *Evolution of Educational Thought* (1977), changes in ideas of knowledge in complex societies and the means by which such ideas are transmitted result from continual struggles among competing groups within society, each of which seeks domination or influence.

The study of the role of men of Islamic learning in Morocco's recent history also raises basic issues concerning the political responsibilities of men of learning, and the relationship between knowledge and political and economic domination. Just as Morocco's rulers necessarily turned to men of learning in the late nineteenth and early twentieth centuries to expand the scope of governmental activities, so did the French once they established their protectorate in 1912. In the first decade of Morocco's colonial era, religious scholars were almost the only Moroccans with full literacy in Arabic. Without the cooptation of men of learning, the colonial regime would not have been able to have expanded rapidly its administrative and taxation apparatus into rural areas.

Moroccan men of learning were opposed to the growing

French encroachment (K. Brown 1972); after direct French intervention, some men of learning and other religious leaders figured prominently in open resistance (Hammoudi 1981). But for the most part, they refrained from direct political involvement, as was earlier the case in neighboring Tunisia (L. C. Brown 1972; Green 1978) and Algeria (Christelow 1982; cf. Merad 1967). Others, recognizing the futility of direct resistance, allowed themselves to be used in "pacification" efforts in order to avert bloodshed. Particularly in rural society, where the overwhelming majority of Moroccans lived,[1] many men of learning, often from families of rural notables, agreed only with reluctance to cooperate with the colonial administration.

"Cooperation" with the French was an effective means of social mobility for many Moroccan notables, especially in the early years of colonial rule. It would be wrong to assume that all such "friends of France" were acting primarily in terms of self-interest, a charge subsequently leveled by many nationalists after Morocco regained its independence. Such interpretation in hindsight by nationalists admittedly explains why many men of learning have remained silent on their role during the colonial era. Some undoubtedly were opportunists. Military intelligence reports written during the first years of French presence in Morocco often suggest that the principal concern of notables was with preserving their wealth and status.[2] Yet these same reports make clear that the French were careful in their contact with notables, especially religious scholars, to stress that the French were acting at the request of the Makhzan in order to bring order and peace to Morocco. This fiction quickly wore thin, but men of learning and other notables recognized that they had no means of directly opposing the French.

[1] In 1914, an estimated 89 percent of Morocco's total population was rural. As late as 1969, 68.5 percent were still so classified, although by the 1960s remittances from emigrant labor began to figure significantly in the rural economy (Noin 1970: 42). In 1980 an estimated 57 percent of Morocco's population was rural (Escallier 1981: 12).

[2] For detailed examples of such reporting, see Eickelman (1976: 211-254).

Moroccan men of learning in the early part of this century resented the colonial presence but felt that the means of recovering Morocco's autonomy was internal renewal and a recommitment to education and discipline. In this reformist "neo-Salafi" view, to adopt Binsa'id's useful term, Islam was the "religion of order" or self-discipline (*dīn al-niẓām*) (Binsa'id 1983: 33). By the late 1940s popular nationalism eclipsed such ideas among a younger generation of educated Moroccans, but it would be wrong to regard such neo-Salafi ideas as no more than precursors of nationalism. I suggest in Chapter Seven that neo-Salafi thought may have more in common with what is generically known today as "resurgent" Islam than with nationalist thought. Many Moroccans remain uneasy in discussing neo-Salafi ideas today because of their implications for "collaboration." Such a blanket interpretation constitutes an anachronistic misreading of an earlier era in which alternative notions of political responsibility prevailed among men of learning, ideas that remain important in defining the attitudes of many Moroccans toward state authority. Just as the French have found it difficult to recount the Vichy era, and for similar reasons, Moroccans have passed over many aspects of colonial rule in silence. Much of this silence is due to the difficulty the generation of Moroccans who experienced the earlier part of this era first-hand have in explaining its subtleties and ironies to those who only know it through the political rhetoric of later times.

INTELLECTUALS: CONTEXT AND STYLE

The Moroccan historian Abdallah Laroui (1977b: 191) argues that Moroccan men of learning in the nineteenth century possessed "the moral influence that legitimates all political action." By the late 1920s they ceased to form the near-totality of educated Moroccans, especially after the children of the elite shifted from the great mosque-universities to the schools established by the French for the sons of notables. The influence of men of learning nonetheless remained significant, especially in the countryside. In the independence movement of the early 1950s, some formed the cadres of rural resistance or actively supported them, especially in the hinterland of Marrakesh. In some regions of southern Morocco in the 1960s, notables who were also men of learning could still win elections simply by standing for them (Leveau 1976: 93, 116, 188-189), although this was no longer the case for many other regions of the country (e.g., Rosen 1979: 50-53).

The relation between prevalent style of religious knowledge carried by the traditionally educated and the wider social context in which such notions are maintained is especially evident in rural Morocco. As a category, men of learning in rural society constituted an important pool from which Morocco's "secondary elite" were drawn, those who allowed the rulers to rule (Mosca 1939). I describe them as a category rather than as a group because the carriers of religious learning are recognized as sharing that attribute alone, and do not constitute a group that acts together politically or in any other way. Indeed, although some men of learning compose an important element of the rural elite, others, such as rural Quranic teachers, do not.

Writing of an admittedly different social and cultural context, Antonio Gramsci (1971: 14-15) considers rural intellectuals to be "organic" in the sense that every development among the peasantry "up to a certain point, is linked to and depends upon movements among the intellectuals." For Gramsci, intellectuals—clerks, judges, teachers, scribes, other professionals, and (my own addition for the Moroccan context) educated merchants—bring the peasantry into contact with the local and state administration. Gramsci argues that intellectuals are few in number in rural society, their command of literacy is understood by few, and their social position is such that it is difficult for them to act independently of the established social order (cf. Schumpeter 1962: 147). Even if rural intellectuals are not directly involved in political administration, it is difficult to separate their various roles as judges, notaries, and clerics from the political milieu. Moreover, the standard of living of rural intellectuals is generally higher than that of much of the rest of the rural population, so that the peasantry looks to the "gentlemanly" rural intellectual as a social model to which at least one of his own sons might aspire. Even if not always resulting in economic advancement, the pursuit of religious knowledge in rural Morocco is seen as a commendable end in itself.

Gramschi's notion of intellectuals in rural society needs comment. Other scholars, notably Edward Shils (1972: 3), characterize intellectuals as persons "with an unusual sensitivity to the sacred, an uncommon reflectiveness about the nature of their universe and the rules which govern their society." An intellectual by this definition need not be confined to the formally educated or to those explicitly engaged in mental work. Nor is it evident that persons engaged in such pursuits as notaries, scribes, and judges lead an "intellectual" life by reason of their profession. Despite Gramschi's choice of terms, his formulation equally approximates the original Russian notion of intelligentsia as the educated class of society, or those to whom "advanced" political or, as in rural Morocco, religious ideas are attributed. Although it is useful to separate the two notions of intellectual and intelligentsia for some purposes, Gramschi's merging of the two notions points to a necessary and significant overlap in contexts where full literacy is possessed only by a minority, as has been the case in Morocco until recent decades (see Chapter Three).

Profound changes are underway in the role of Islamic learning and of its carriers in Moroccan society and in other Islamic countries, although, given the lack until recently of scholarly attention to contemporary Islamic learning, it has been difficult to trace these changes in detail. Only within the last decade (esp. Akhavi 1980; Fischer 1980a, 1980b, 1982), has there been renewed interest in the subject. In the case of Morocco, an interest in contemporary Islamic learning was sustained almost alone for many years by a talented colonial administrator, who subsequently became an academic at the end of the colonial era (Berque 1938, 1974). Scholarly interest in the theme was marginal.

A compelling reason for the benign scholarly neglect of "traditional" intellectuals is that there was no clear place for them in prevailing assumptions concerning the role of intellectuals in contemporary societies. Abdallah Laroui (1967: 19-28), for example, divides contemporary Arab intellectuals into three main categories, a triad implicit in the writings of many other Arab intellectuals. First are the clerics, the religious intellectuals who seek a definition of society and the means to its improvement in religious ideology. Second are the politician-liberals, who seek the betterment of society through adopting political forms inspired largely by the West. Technocrats constitute a third broad category encompassing everything from militant Marxists to "apolitical," Western-educated advocates of social engineering. Despite other differences, intellectuals in this category share the conviction that society can be improved largely through "rational" means that require minimal attention to their society's specific cultural heritage.

Laroui's argument that each of these three intellectual styles has predominated in successive historical contexts is problematical. It ignores the progressive differentiation of intellectual styles and orientations that has taken place in the twentieth century. These intellectual styles coexist in the contemporary Middle East and, as indicated by Laroui's repeated and appropriate invocation of the experience of his native Morocco, often overlap in intricate ways.

In contrast to Laroui's sharp delineation of politican-liberals and technocrats, his category of "cleric," the most complex of the three, is the most vaguely delineated and residual. Fischer (1982: 108), more immediately concerned with contemporary clerics, delineates five major clerical orientations in Iran, each with differing ideological and organizational implications. Fischer's categorization is more effective than Laroui's, at least for Iran, in suggesting the wide spectrum of available and emerging religious ideologies and orientations to action, ranging from "reformist" ideologies that require active persuasion to win adherents and that represent a break with the status quo, to notions that profoundly resonate with popular, existing religious understandings.

Of Laroui's categories, the clerics are for the most part also less interested than the carriers of the other two intellectual styles in pursuing dialogues with Westerners or with Western-educated scholars. As Albert Hourani (1970: viii) wrote in the first reissue of *Arabic Thought in the Liberal Age*, most studies of Arab intellectuals, including his own, "did not say enough" about those who rejected or disregarded "the dominant ideas of modern Europe." The resulting miscomprehension of Iranian society requires no further reiteration, but in other countries there has been a similar neglect of the influence of the traditionally educated. In the case of Afghanistan, Ashraf Ghani argues that the traditionally educated intellectuals, many of whom today have also had some education in state-sponsored educational institutions, continue to play an important role in shaping attitudes toward modernism and the west.[3] The publication of the works of a fourteenth-century theologian, Ibn Taymiyya, can stir major intellectual and political controversy in Egypt in the 1980s (Sivan 1983). "Traditional" intellectuals place a particular value upon the past, but are not necessarily locked into the past. Intellectual traditions can undergo major changes that their carriers do not regard as such (Shils 1981: 14). I argue that this has been the case with Islamic "clerics."

The notion of contemporary clerics as a residual category equally pervades the influential work of Edward Shils. For Shils, intellectuals possess an "innate need" to be in "frequent communion with symbols which are more general than the immediate concrete situations of everyday life" (Shils 1972: 16). Although intellectual work originally arose from religious occupations, Shils writes that religious orientations in modern times attract "a diminishing share of the creative capacities

[3] Personal communication, May 31, 1983.

of the oncoming intellectual elite" (ibid.). In Shils' view, among Western intellectuals in earlier periods, and Asian and African intellectuals since the nineteenth century, "the tradition of distrust of secular and ecclesiastical authority—and in fact of tradition as such—has become the chief secondary tradition of the intellectuals" (1972: 17). The notion of the sacred has shifted in his view from religious concerns to a focus upon and mastery of the technological, organizational, and political skills most useful in forging a modern state in the face of congeries of primordial loyalties. In terms of Laroui's categories, the present belongs to the liberals and the technocrats. Shils argues that in the contemporary world, intellectuals are found primarily in the differentiated "modern" class. He argues that only intellectuals attached to "modern" values have the vision to rise above parochial identities and to attach themselves to the notion of a modern nation-state.

Shils notwithstanding, traditionally educated Islamic intellectuals also emphasize identities that are far from parochial, even if not wholly congruent with the technocratic and "liberal" vision of what is needed to maintain a modern nation-state. Unfortunately, the notion of an all-important "modern" category of intellectuals that accompanied the heyday of modernization theory in the 1950s reinforced the tendency to treat clerics as a residual or disappearing category on the margin of significant political activity. As a practical reminder of this attitude, a reviewer for a proposal I wrote in the mid-1970s commented that it had merit only as history, not as anthropology, for "traditional" Islamic intellectuals throughout the Middle East were isolated, dying old men with no significant influence upon contemporary events. There are specifically anthropological precedents for the study of intellectuals and intellectual traditions elsewhere in the world (e.g., Griaule 1965; Radin 1957; Turner 1967: 131-150), but not for the Middle East. Only the 1978-1979 Iranian revolution returned to the center stage of social thought a tradition that has remained vigorous, if not always politically dominant.

ONE

Biography as a Social Document

BECAUSE of its complexity, Moroccan society lends itself to the use of biographies as a means of understanding wider social and political realities. Two talented journalists (Lacouture and Lacouture 1958) portrayed the key social and political forces of the period leading to Morocco's independence through biographical profiles of major French and Moroccan political figures. Jacques Berque's (1958) account of the seventeenth-century religious scholar Sidi al-Ḥasan al-Yūsī (1631-1691), who also figures prominently in Clifford Geertz's *Islam Observed* (1968a), depicts the intellectual and religious milieu of a crucial era in Moroccan history. A political scientist (Waterbury 1972) has used the life of a prominent Sūsī merchant in Casablanca to exemplify the economic and political sensibilities of an entire generation, and anthropologists have used biographies as devices to analyze such diverse topics as possession states (Crapanzano 1980), the nature of ethnography and the ethnographic encounter (Crapanzano 1980; Dwyer 1982), family relationships (Munson 1984), and political and "cultural" alienation (Rabinow 1975). Each of these studies succeeds to the extent that it convincingly depicts major social and cultural issues. Yet, for English-speaking readers, the notion of biography immediately evokes a Victorian genre for which, because its primary audience is assumed to share a common cultural heritage and knowledge of historical context, more general issues are often raised only obliquely.

The study presented here is intended as a social biography. By focusing upon the training, career, and moral imagination of a rural qadi, it reduces the familiar notion of the "docu-

14

mentary method" to its minimal form. Clifford Geertz, who traces the notion through Harold Garfinkel and Karl Mannheim, characterizes this approach as the interpretation of

> ... a single naturally coherent social phenomenon ... a specific manifestation of a more comprehensive pattern which has a very large, in some cases virtually infinite, number of such embodiments and manifestations, the one at hand simply being regarded as particularly telling in the fullness, the clarity, and the elegance with which it exhibits the general pattern (Geertz 1965: 153-154).

Social biographies, called life histories by some anthropologists, are often considered to be closer to raw data than analytical presentations. The distinction between the anecdotal and the social document is often unclear. Yet as an analytic device, the social document can be an effective means of exploring uncharted territory (Young 1983: 479-480). In Islamic studies, Louis Massignon (1982) uses a biography of the Sufi al-Ḥallāj (858-922) as a point of departure for a comprehensive discussion of Islamic mysticism. In this study, I use a social biographical approach to break accepted stereotypes held both by Westerners and by many Middle Easterners themselves of Islamic learning and its carriers.

I use the term social biography rather than life history to emphasize that this narrative does not purport to be a vehicle to allow a Berber qāḍī, Ḥājj 'Abd ar-Raḥmān Manṣūrī, a friend and consociate thirty years my senior, to speak for himself. His voice is present throughout the text, but so is mine. A significant part of this account is the result of extended dialogues in some respects like those contained in Marcel Griaule's *Conversations with Ogotêmmeli* (1965). Unlike Griaule's narrative, which is primarily a one-way representation of indigenous thought, this account incorporates multiple voices, especially that of the ethnographer. An awareness of multiple voices is, I think, essential to understanding the nature of the anthropological encounter today (cf. Geertz 1968b). The ethnographer's presence is almost invisible in a monograph such as Evans-Pritchard's *The Nuer* (1940) or even in "autobiographical" narratives such as those presented by Oscar Lewis (1961); in some recent ethnographies the self-reflexivity of the ethnographer, concerned about the "power relationships" of the ethnographic encounter, almost preclude further ethnographic analysis. I think that ethnography involves a balance between the two extremes. As the qadi and I worked together, we both became aware of our differences in understanding how events could be narrated and interpreted, of what was said and what was left out. These differences became part of the record of interpretation. Through my questions and his, we became mutually aware and appreciative of our respective intellectual projects. When I first became acquainted with the qadi, I was barely aware of this dimension of ethnographic understanding. Especially in the heydey of structuralist analysis in the 1960s, ethnographic analysis had been conveyed to me as a priestly tradition in which the conscious understanding of "natives" or their efforts at understanding their own society played a minimal role.

The decision to portray the social context of Islamic knowledge in rural Morocco through the social biography of a living qadi is in part fortuitous. Hajj 'Abd ar-Rahman was born in 1912 in Bzū, a small Berber town in the foothills of the High Atlas mountains. After studying in Bzu and its environs, learning to speak Arabic in the process, he went in 1928 to the famed Yusufiya mosque-university in Marrakesh, where he remained until 1935. Then his politically minded elder brother, by then the qadi of Bzu, cut short his studies in order to have him appointed as Bzu's deputy qadi.

I met Hajj 'Abd ar-Rahman during my first field research in Morocco (1968-1970). He was then qadi of Boujad, the regional pilgrimage center in which I had chosen to work. He was also my landlord. Only toward the end of my first stay in Morocco did the idea of specifically writing about his life begin to take shape. I first broached the idea to him in late 1969, although in reviewing my notes prior to then I find

extensive entries related to his personal experiences, perceptions, and participation in the events of this century. At first
I regarded these discussions to be on the margins of my primary work on Boujad, since the Hajj was from elsewhere in
Morocco. Nonetheless, I recorded them as systematically as
I did all my field notes, as soon after discussions as possible,
in order to preserve the texture of the original discussions. At
his request, we never used a tape recorder; he regarded the
device as breaking the confidentiality of discussion. In any
case, when I failed to understand a point developed in my
notes, we could return to it later. The extensive record of our
discussions was completed before I raised the possibility of
writing specifically on him, and has served as an excellent
check on whether he subsequently shaped his narrative and
presentation of self to accommodate his new role as the subject
of a book. Because of his notion of presentation of self, discussed in detail later in this chapter, I think that such distortion
has been minimal.

I subsequently returned to Morocco several times (summers
of 1972, 1973, 1976, 1978, 1981 and 1984). Each time I took
the opportunity to work further with Hajj 'Abd ar-Rahman
and to interview other scholars and associates of his who were
at the Yusufiya. The task was made easier by the fact that he
had kept a diary and assorted personal papers since the early
1930s, though they were in part destroyed for fear of reprisals
during the colonial era, and the diary was not, in the Western
sense, a systematic, cumulative record of personal events and
experiences. It was episodic, recording only those actions and
events that to him formed "history." The fact that it was not
a Western-style diary was in itself significant. It provided a
document which, although it was his creation, was independent of the two of us and could be used as a point of departure
for interpretation.

I agree with Laroui when he observes that of his three types
of Arab intellectuals, the "clerics" are those least interested
in communicating with Western scholars. Yet he also notes
that the foreign scholar has, at least at the outset, certain

advantages over the indigenous one, especially in the study of elites. As an outsider, the foreign scholar is less suspect of participating in local rivalries and thus is more likely to secure cooperation (Laroui 1977b: 15). As a "stranger" (Simmel 1964) at the outset, the foreigner is also obliged to ask basic questions about the nature of the social world that "natives" are supposed to know and therefore do not or cannot ordinarily discuss with one another.

I shared at least part of 'Abd ar-Rahman's social world on a long-term, first-hand basis for two years in Boujad. During this time, in company with him and on my own, I also met many of his friends and fellow administrators in visits throughout western Morocco, Marrakesh, and its hinterland. In subsequent returns to Morocco, after I had specifically decided to write about 'Abd ar-Rahman and traditional Islamic learning, I built upon these existing ties and developed others.

Some Moroccan men of learning discouraged me from writing about a rural qadi. They felt that I should invest my time in studying the pinnacle of erudition as they conceived it, and argued that the life of a country judge would provide me with a distorted, impoverished image of Islamic learning. My response was to observe that Moroccan men of learning themselves were much better situated than I was to interpret trends in the body of Islamic knowledge as it is understood and developed in Morocco today. My own intent was instead to focus upon the contexts in which such knowledge was learned, elaborated, and reproduced, and how it was valued in society at large. Once some men of learning realized that my intent was not to replicate Islamic knowledge as they alone could understand it, they agreed that the world of traditional learning about which I chose to write was rapidly becoming unfamiliar even to a younger generation of Moroccans, so that there might be some value in my scholarly project after all. Perhaps some merely appeared to acquiesce in my rationale because they saw there was no point in dissuading me, although the tenor of questions suggested a clear understanding of my project, if not always acceptance of it. The fact that my initially "unfamiliar" goals could be comprehended and respected by traditional men of learning, especially those who had little to do with foreigners or the foreign-educated, re-affirmed for me the openness and flexibility of the world of traditional Islamic learning, attributes not generally accorded to it by those who observe it from a distance.

THE ANTHROPOLOGIST AND THE JUDGE

In November 1968, once I decided to work in Boujad, I had the difficult task of finding a place to live. In the company of an impoverished tribesman who had recently settled in Boujad in order to become an underemployed tailor, I spent several chilled, drizzly days on foot in Boujad, looking at dozens of houses that my wife and I heard might be available for rent. With the exception of an English missionary who had been in Boujad since the late 1930s, no foreigner ever chose to live in the old quarters (*madīna*). The few French teachers assigned to Boujad were spatially segregated in bungalows next to the administrative center, and kept largely to themselves, social-izing only minimally with their Moroccan colleagues. Ade-quate housing was scarce, and my insistence upon living in the madina was viewed as odd. Local government officials, who to their credit were indifferent to my presence rather than hostile, were not prepared to offer any suggestions. They sim-ply did not know how to handle foreigners who did not fall into the accepted pattern of self-segregation. As I trudged through the madina, it was depressing to be offered everything from houses with caved-in second stories ("Just step around the hole in the floor, and it's a fine apartment") to one vacant for a decade because it was said to be occupied by jinn ("They shouldn't affect *you*"). In retrospect, I obtained a very good idea of the traditional quarters and was informally introduced to a number of merchants and residents. At the time, however, the sheer bleakness of available housing weighed more heavily upon me. Finally, at dusk on the third day, just before the sunset prayers, I was led to the house of the qadi.

Over tea, the qadi questioned me at length about my work and had me translate into Arabic my official Moroccan letter of introduction, written in French. He then left us to say his sunset prayers at the neighborhood mosque. When he returned, he said that he was willing to rent us his empty two-room apartment across the street.

So Hajj 'Abd ar-Rahman Mansuri became our landlord. As the notable of our quarter, Darb Zalāghī, he was impeccably hospitable to my wife and me. Due to my own inexperience, our relations were nonetheless rocky at first. For instance, we had a misunderstanding on the electricity bill, which he had agreed to pay until it became clear that our working habits made us major consumers. Then, a month later, I was at home recovering from anthrax (an unexpected fringe hazard of field research), when a workman suddenly began removing our windows from the outside in order to brick up the openings. Our landlord had not informed us that he was building a second house abutting our own. Work was suspended until I had recovered, but the fact that we were not informed about his building plans and had to endure the noise from months of intermittent construction did not please us. I fortunately vented most, but not all, of my petulance only in my field notes.

In January 1969, I began regularly to attend the weekly sessions of the Islamic court (*maḥkamat ash-shrā'*) held each Thursday, the day of Boujad's weekly market. The court handled all matters pertaining to marriage, divorce, support, inheritance, and land transactions subject to Islamic law. Because court business in Boujad itself was light, Hajj 'Abd ar-Rahman had become a Moroccan circuit rider. On rotating days of the week, his one-armed bailiff drove him to other courts in the region: Wād Zam, Qaṣba Tādla, and Bnī Millāl.

Sometimes I accompanied Hajj 'Abd ar-Rahman on his rounds, but it was easier to follow court proceedings in Boujad than elsewhere. Until the mid-1970s, when a new building was constructed by the Ministry of Justice, sessions were held in a small room in the former colonial administrative center (*contrôle*), constructed in 1931. The only furnishings in the room beside a telephone (one of some thirty in Boujad) were a rickety table with three chairs, for the judge, his clerk, and (when I was present) the anthropologist. Litigants sat on a narrow wooden bench about ten feet long, situated about six feet in front of the qadi's table. Except for myself, no spectators were allowed. Litigants waited their turn outside or followed proceedings from the windows.

The modern courts in larger towns, designed by French architects, were much more august and spacious, with imposing desks for judges on an elevated dais. Litigants were kept up to twenty feet away. Much as in an American court, a large number of spectators were accommodated on rows of wooden benches with backrests. In such conditions, it was difficult to follow proceedings. In part this was because of poor acoustics, but it was also because many spectators spoke in low voices to one another while awaiting the case of particular interest to them. The spatial design and presence of spectators also imposed a formality on the proceedings not present in the Boujad court.

In Boujad, the qadi decided that I must sit with him and his clerk, since I could not sit with the litigants. I always moved my chair to the edge of the table to indicate that I was not part of the proceedings. Nonetheless some tribesmen unfamiliar with court procedures recognized me as a foreigner and sometimes saluted, perhaps assuming that a small pocket of colonial influence survived independence in 1956. Others paid scant regard to me. With writing-pad before me, I was taken to be another clerk. Litigants would rise and try to move even closer when proceedings got heated. One task of the bailiff, usually armed with a cane, was to push them back. The qadi had worked with his baliff and one of the two rotating clerks for years, so that there was an easy working relationship among the court officers.

For each court case, litigants had to engage a notary to

prepare a deposition. Since notaries charge by the page for such documents, many had little concern as to whether claims and counterclaims had legal validity or even fell within the jurisdiction of the court. The qadi took a few moments to study these documents. If the claim was properly prepared and fell within the scope of the court, a summary of it was dictated into the record by the qadi. The qadi put questions to the litigants to verify the facts of each case. A summary of questions and his decision were then dictated in classical Arabic, accompanied by citation of the appropriate sections of the Moroccan personal status code.[1]

Few tribesmen could follow the proceedings. When the facts of a case had to be clarified through questioning, the litigants more often than not tried to recite the entire history of the dispute, which was extremely useful to me but not to the court. The qadi usually put his questions in colloquial Arabic. Since the verdict, however, was given in classical Arabic, litigants often were unaware of the decision. The judge left it to the bailiff to "translate" the verdict into colloquial speech, which he often did by pointing to litigants and saying, "You won! You lost!" and ushering them, confused and protesting, out of the room.

In contrast, the qadi welcomed my interest in court proceedings. Because the Boujad court calendar was usually uncrowded, Hajj 'Abd ar-Rahman often took a few minutes between cases to explain to me the legal issues involved and what the litigants were trying to accomplish. Often he knew the background to the cases from sources outside of the court. Many litigants, especially townspeople, often sought his advice outside of formal court sessions in order to avoid court proceedings.

When I first began to attend these sessions, 'Abd ar-Rahman and his clerks tested my understanding of the proceedings. They were difficult to follow, but my prior training in classical Arabic was useful: I knew much of the legal terminology, and

[1] See Rosen (1980) for a formal analysis of Moroccan Islamic law courts.

the legal issues involved were rarely complicated. The major initial problem in anthropological inquiry is how to get people to explain their perception of events as they would to an "insider" (Merton 1972). The most valuable anthropological work begins once people take for granted a shared appreciation of the issues at hand, although these "background" perceptions are usually the most difficult to elicit. Some people, including Hajj 'Abd ar-Rahman, began to see not only that I knew more than I could readily explain but that there was a pattern to my questions and started to take an interest in them.

Regular attendance at the court meant that I soon learned the issues involved. I began to ask questions that "insiders" could conceivably ask. If I learned that someone had brought the same case to the court in 1960, I would ask how the 1960 case differed from the 1968 one. This type of question engendered specific responses, usually laced with other practical examples indicating how the use of courts was but one element in the resolution of grievances. If, on the other hand, I asked an abstract question about property or inheritance rights, Hajj 'Abd ar-Rahman's response was usually as formal and devoid of realistic context as the initial question.

Thursday and Friday were the social high points of the week for Boujad's notables. On Thursdays they held major lunches for one another and for tribal clients who had come in for the market. Lunches were also held on Fridays, after the prayers and sermon in the principal mosque. After court, the qadi often invited me to accompany him, so I regularly saw notables who were otherwise indifferent to my presence. Ordinary conversations concerned real estate and market transactions, and cryptic local gossip not openly explained to me. With my notebook often near at hand, I may have appealed to Hajj 'Abd ar-Rahman as a poor man's Boswell and obliquely lent him status. When I put questions to him directly, he seemed pleased to live up to his reputation as a man of learning and speak "high words," quotations from the Quran and classical Arabic literature. Sometimes he used a discussion with me as a polite way of extricating himself from other conversations. In any case, I was tolerated, and pretended to understand and appreciate more of his quotations from legal texts and Andalusian poets than I, or most of the others present, could readily assimilate.

I rarely saw Hajj 'Abd ar-Rahman alone during the first months of our stay in Boujad. In March 1969, he invited my wife and me to travel with him to Bzu, his village of birth, where I met his elder brother, Aḥmad Manṣūrī, for the first time. I knew of his elder brother's reputation for Islamic learning, but I was still unaware that there were interesting questions to ask concerning the role of Islamic learning and that it was as necessary to understanding Islam in Moroccan society as were the maraboutic practices that were then at the center of my research (Eickelman 1976). Maraboutism was the prevalent popular belief that certain persons, living or dead, possess a special relation toward God which makes them particularly well placed to act as intermediaries and to communicate God's grace (*baraka*) to their clients. This implicit belief was in uncomfortable tension with Islam as understood by educated Moroccans and many townsmen. Tribesmen from throughout western Morocco annually visited Boujad because of the presence there of major shrines, and the town's religious, political and economic leadership had until recent times been held largely by members of the Sharqāwī maraboutic descent group.

Understanding these popular religious beliefs and historical change in them was in itself a complex, engrossing task. My attitude at the time was that visiting with rural notables in other parts of Morocco provided me with an interesting break in routine and an opportunity to set my own intensive work in Boujad and the Tadla plain in an appropriate wider context. I could not possibly master the nuances of local political detail for other regions, and I had not yet realized the significance of formal Islamic learning and its carriers in establishing important transregional links.

THE SHARQAWI PAPERS

In June 1969 my conception of what was important and possible in field research changed abruptly through one of the accidents common to anthropological fieldwork. Since the late nineteenth century, the Sharqāwa of Boujad, the maraboutic descent group that I was studying, had been divided into two major factions, made all the more permanent when the French conferred the title of qadi upon the leader of one and *qā'id*, meaning in this case an urban chieftainship, upon the leader of the other (Eickelman 1976: 196-202, 239-254). At the beginning of the Protectorate in 1912, the office of qaid looked like the more significant of the two (Cimitière 1913). Yet by the 1940s it became clear that this office, more than that of qadi, was compromised through collaboration with the French. Its attentions were devoted almost exclusively to local concerns, and its leaders proved unprepared to adapt constructively to Morocco's changing political circumstances.

Unlike the faction and descent group allied with the qaid, members of the faction awarded the "consolation" of the qadiship invested heavily in education and moved to Rabat and Casablanca. Some of its members were early participants in the nationalist movement. The marriage of a prominent member of this faction to the daughter of King Muḥammad bin Yūsif (Muhammad V) (r. 1927-1961) shortly after independence, and his subsequent appointment to ministerial and ambassadorial posts, assured the eclipse of the other faction.

In the first month of my stay in Boujad, I met one of the notables of the "Zāwiya" Sharqāwa, as the faction that formerly held the qaidship was locally called. He showed me a cache of documents, most of which dated from the late nineteenth and early twentieth centuries, related to Sharqawi leaders and their ties with tribes, merchants, Morocco's rulers, and the French. He assumed at the time that I had no command of written Arabic. I was supposed to admire the calligraphy and the seals of various sultans. When it became clear that I could also read the documents, they were quietly eased away from me. I was repeatedly assured that I could study them later, but as the months passed an excuse was always found not to produce them.

In the meantime my wife, who also speaks Arabic, had developed cordial ties with some of the women of the notable's household. Contrary to popular stereotypes, some Moroccan women are quite independent and decide household matters themselves (Davis 1983). My wife mentioned my interest in seeing the documents and the fact that I had been assured access to them. Somewhat to her surprise, one day they were produced without fuss, and I had them on loan for several months.

There were some six hundred documents in all. Some concerned marriage contracts and inheritance. Others were letters to and from various Sharqawi leaders concerning such topics as revenues from estates, pilgrimage income, safe conducts and the release of prisoners, local and national politics, and relations with French military intelligence. Collectively the documents provided an intimate view of the practical operations of a religious lodge during the tumultuous final years before the protectorate.

The notarial script of most of the documents was excruciatingly difficult for me to read, and the nibblings of mice at many of the documents did not facilitate my task. I engaged a local notary ('adl) to dictate them into a tape recorder. Even with this help, the language of the documents was difficult and depended for interpretation upon a knowledge of the personalities and unrecorded local events of the period.

I assumed at the outset that Hajj 'Abd ar-Rahman was too busy with other matters to be concerned with my inquiries, but I asked one of his sons, an excellent student then in secondary school, to assist me with the letters. Every few days he took some letters home and returned with meticulous transcriptions into ordinary Arabic script, as opposed to the difficult notarial one, and reasonably accurate translations into French. I was impressed by his apparent ease in deciphering notarial script and explaining the letters. One day I asked him to assist me on the spot with a document on which I had been working alone. He then casually told me that he couldn't read the script either. His father had actually been doing the work.

Just before the sunset prayers that very evening, I noticed the qadi himself standing on the street outside our apartment. Men of the neighborhood often gathered outside the small mosque adjoining our apartment before and after the evening prayers, but the qadi rarely joined them for long. Moreover, this evening he was alone. I guessed that he wanted to see me. I went out to the street to join him, exchanged courtesies, and as if by chance showed him a few of the documents. He smiled and immediately invited me to his house.

That evening we began a series of meetings that went on for three months, until Hajj 'Abd ar-Rahman's unexpected transfer to neighboring Wad Zam in September 1969. Depending on his schedule and mine, we met daily for as long as six hours. On days when his official schedule was full, he eliminated his customary afternoon nap in favor of our work. Sometimes we began after a light supper and continued until midnight. After our first few meetings, he ordered his family and servants to say that he was not in if anyone called who could be sent away. When he was unavoidably called away, he left me by myself in one room and dealt quickly with the caller. His excitement in working with the documents was transparent and contagious.

His interest in the documents was complex. After our first month of work, he showed me notebooks he had prepared when he was first assigned as a qadi to Boujad in 1957. The Sharqawa had owned agricultural estates in Bzu since the eighteenth century, so Hajj 'Abd ar-Rahman had prior familiarity with some Sharqawi notables. Nonetheless, his notebooks showed that he had faced the same initial difficulty as I had in tracing out the intricate ties of local kinship and patronage. Whenever he had come across marriage contracts or inheritance documents in the course of his work which clarified Sharqawi interconnections, he had recorded their rel-

FIGURE 2. The Anthropologist and the Qadi, 1969.
The photograph is posed at the qadi's request.
Hence the bound volume in his hands.

evant details in his notebooks. Since his arrival in Boujad, he
had been aware of the existence of the documents we were
now studying, but he was never given an opportunity to see
them. I subsequently learned that the notable holding the documents, himself unable to read them properly, feared that
some papers might have a bearing upon current inheritance
disputes; none did.

Making sense of the "Sharqawi papers" was exciting but
grueling work. Cohn (1981: 247) writes of the rise in recent
years of an "anthropological history" whose goal is to "grasp
the meanings of the forms and contents of texts and codified
oral traditions in their own cultural terms" instead of as reflections of European history (see also Becker and Yengoyan
1979). I was learning to follow the contours of an "indigenous
form of knowledge" in a manner that was as rewarding as
the interviews I was conducting in other contexts. Moreover,
I was working side by side with a "native" scholar, then in
his late fifties, with his own fully developed perspective on
how to interpret the documents.

The terms, concepts, and social world evoked by these documents were at first bewildering. The style in which Hajj 'Abd ar-Rahman related events was likewise difficult to comprehend, and I began to realize that understanding how he interpreted historical documents and learned to do so would in itself be an important component of our common work.

As WE sorted through the mass of documents, Hajj 'Abd ar-Rahman made linkages between persons, incidents, and property of which I was at first only dimly aware. Of equal importance, I needed innumerable glosses on the evaluative terms invoked by the qadi in order to understand the significance of the papers. For instance, the qadi would refer to the style and calligraphy of a particular Sharqawi as "common" ('āmmī). I knew the term of course, and the notable/commoner (nās khāṣṣa/'awām) distinction which was invoked in a variety of contexts, often on the basis of claimed descent in Boujad. Hajj 'Abd ar-Rahman usually used the term to distinguish between those who were educated and those who were not. My questions, intended to confirm my understanding of this distinction, led to a concrete discussion on the nuances of writing and how the "educated" perceived historical events. We discussed such topics as the contexts in which the various documents were originally written, the importance of calligraphic style to men of learning, and why there is no terminological distinction among men of learning between biography and autobiography, both known as tarjama (pl. tarājim). I was being given a practical introduction to the rhetorical style valued among men of learning and how it was acquired.

Often I was astonished at 'Abd ar-Rahman's assiduity in extracting full meaning from every document. Marriage contracts were one such subset of the documents. He knew enough of the background of the persons involved, often long deceased, to suggest why a certain marriage may have occurred. Or, quite frequently, he would make discreet inquiries of other persons to confirm his speculations. On one occasion,

I was present at a luncheon with a Sharqawi notable when the qadi worked a question concerning some nearly forgotten marriage into his conversation, then feigning disinterest so as not to arouse too much curiosity. He carefully separated his own assumption of motives from "real" history, which to him was a reliable record of actual speech and action.

Hajj ʿAbd ar-Rahman enjoyed work on the Sharqawi papers as much as I did. An enumeration of the property included in the bridewealth (ṣdāq) of a marriage in the 1890s enabled Hajj ʿAbd ar-Rahman, prompted by my questions, to organize his own thoughts (and information sometimes scattered in his notebooks) on the rural economy of an earlier period, caravan routes and their organizers, and the Makhzan's varying practical scope. During one of our sessions, I recall setting aside a document because in my judgment it had served too long as a rodent snack to be of further value. Hajj ʿAbd ar-Rahman was not so easily deterred. From the date, the handwriting, and a few decipherable phrases he was able convincingly to explain to me how the letter was related to more complete documents we had already seen.

Almost any topic triggered a systematic introduction to another domain of knowledge and practice. One day, entering his courtyard, I saw a number of men's tunics (jallābas) being sunned. I had not previously sought to distinguish among them, and casually asked the provenance of one. The result was an hour's discussion of the origins of particular materials, regional styles and how they were linked to different claims to status, how they were obtained and distributed, and the progressive impact in his lifetime of European textiles upon their production and manufacture.

Despite a difference of thirty years in our ages and radically disparate backgrounds—for my part I was not born a Berber-speaking Muslim nor educated to be a qadi—we began to regard one another as colleagues because of our work on a common project. Hajj ʿAbd ar-Rahman's Boujad notebooks indicated his own ethnographic efforts. My own notes were better than his in terms of explaining general patterns of relationships. He was fascinated that this could be so, given the thinness of my understandings of local conventions in other respects. He was especially fascinated by the information codified in my yards-long charts of Sharqawi family ties and later his own. He knew far more local and regional history and could relate it quite intelligibly to his peers, although I had a decided advantage in interpreting local social history for a wider audience. We learned from one another and we both were aware of the fact.

I also learned the art of framing delicate questions from Hajj 'Abd ar-Rahman. As we worked on the Sharqawi papers, he began to see more clearly a pattern in the issues I pursued with other people. Sometimes he would lend a hand. Late in my initial period of field research I tackled the sensitive issue of resistance against the French in neighboring Wad Zam, the scene of a bloody uprising in August 1955. It was instigated by the Wlād 'Īsa section of the Smā'la tribe; ninety-five French colons were killed in the course of a morning. Colonial authorities were shocked at the strength of this rural uprising. They had come to assume that militant resistance to colonial rule was predominantly urban.

'Abd ar-Rahman and I had accepted an invitation of a local notable to lunch. A tribesman from the Wlad 'Isa had somehow invited himself along. Our host, an influential landowner and notary, was visibly annoyed. He made jokes at the expense of the tribesman and his illiteracy. The tribesman made no reply. Later, I asked him if he knew anything of the 1955 "event." He replied that he had participated. From his distant corner of the long guest room—he was placed near the last in seating order—he began to give me a detailed account. In order to hear him better, I changed places.

At first the others ignored us, but I noticed that Hajj 'Abd ar-Rahman was listening. Soon the room was quiet except for the tribesman. I confined my questions to those necessary to follow his narrative. Few tribesmen were anxious to speak about that event. The version given to the French and, later, to Moroccan officials (who regard the Sma'la as a "rough" tribe to govern because they stand up to local government officials) was that the tribesmen had come to Wad Zam with peaceful intentions but subsequently "lost their heads," having been stirred up by unidentified "outside agitators." In this convenient formulation the question of leadership was muted. Imprecise stereotypes of a "collective" tribal mentality could be invoked to obscure individual responsibility. A week after the event, after the Foreign Legion conservatively estimated that it has killed 300 "rebels" in Wad Zam (then a town of 12,000, including 800 foreigners prior to the massacre) and another 200 in the surrounding region, a by then anachronistic collective sacrifice (t'argība) of twelve bulls was offered to the commander of the French forces to secure an amnesty (amān). At the end of the commander's speech granting pardon, a squadron of military planes overflew the assembly to signify, wrote Le Monde's reporter, French might.[2] In the twilight of Morocco's colonial era, the incident was closed, and Wad Zam's one claim to world attention faded into oblivion.

Throughout the tribesman's narrative, 'Abd ar-Rahman was silent. Then he quietly asked, "Did you come armed?" Ordinarily the Sma'la would not have done so. "Yes," was the answer. It did not occur to me to ask the question directly, and most Moroccans were afraid to ask. The question took the tribesman by surprise, as the qadi later told me it was intended. His one-word answer suggested prior intent, and upset the standard recital of events. Then we started the narrative all over. From what followed, it was clear that the tribal incursion was not only locally organized, but that there was a pattern in the killing that implied an attempt to identify specific targets: Wad Zam was a hotbed of the Présence française, a militant settler anti-nationalist movement with its own record of assassinations and injustice.

I think that the tribesman deliberately made his account gruesome as a way of repaying the rudeness of our host. It took a special act of the sociological imagination to see how

---

[2] Le Monde, August 26, 1955, p. 3, and August 28-29, 1955, pp. 1-2.

the massacre of ninety-five civilians appeared from the vantage of an enthusiastic participant. Hajj ʿAbd ar-Rahman later told me that the narrative of the bloody events of that day upset him considerably. Like myself, he sought to maintain a neutral countenance in order to hear the man out. The tribesman, however, always greeted me like an old friend whenever I saw him after that.

MUCH of what I describe in this book was learned from Hajj ʿAbd ar-Rahman himself. He necessarily served as my guide to the stacks of unsorted papers and notebooks which he had kept since his student days at the Yusufiya. In the course of return visits to Morocco, especially in 1976, I managed to see much of what remained of the Yusufiya mosque-university milieu and of key persons associated with it. I was given access to some of the old student lodgings and the mosques where lesson-circles were held. I met many persons who knew Hajj ʿAbd ar-Rahman and his family, and who assisted me in placing this particular family of rural notables in a wider social and intellectual context.

Work with ʿAbd ar-Rahman quickly shattered my prior assumptions as to the "static" nature of Islamic education. His ability to question persons and interpret documents and to render intelligible complex patterns of social history impressed me. I attributed much of his spirit of critical inquiry to the early upbringing and educational tradition in which he was shaped, and began to consider this tradition, at least as it survived in Morocco through the 1930s, to be as vital as my own tradition of learning aspired to be. ʿAbd ar-Rahman was, I think, aware of my attitude.

I had previously uncritically assumed, for I had been so taught, that the special knowledge possessed by Moroccan men of learning was essentially fixed, remote from everyday life, and artificial, loosely tacked on to the implicit assumptions by which Moroccans shaped their social world and made sense of it. I began to realize how much the world of learning was an integral part of Moroccan life, this world began to

feel less remote to me. I asked Hajj 'Abd ar-Rahman systematically about his own family, upbringing, and education.
Having worked closely with him on the Sharqawi papers, I
was again initially attributed with more understanding than
I had actually attained. Many of my questions were unfamiliar. Given my own perceptions of what constituted essential
knowledge, they compelled him to go beyond the formal presentation of self (as in the tarjama) common to men of learning. His sense of history, perceptions of status, attitudes toward knowledge, and the responsibilities of men of learning
toward fellow Muslims and society were issues that I felt I
could understand only with a more complete idea of his own
experience. By then he again had confidence that there was a
pattern to my questions (to my mind often a diffuse one) and
trusted me to deal with his answers with appropriate discretion.

Once, when I returned to Morocco alone in 1976, he gave
me a key to his house and specifically told me that I should
enter without knocking. It appeared that the only way my
presence could be assimilated was to treat me (and my wife
on subsequent return visits) as part of his own household. As
I typed notes in one of the multipurpose rooms of his house,
the women of the household sometimes entered alone and
unself-consciously spoke with me. The fact that they could
do so affirmed that I was quite literally taken to be part of
the household.

The Mansuri household as I knew it through the mid-1970s
was a warm and intense one. Most of the children have now
moved elsewhere in Morocco to pursue their studies or to set
up households of their own, although one son, a schoolteacher
also involved in local politics, has chosen to remain in Boujad.
The Hajj and his wife, Lalla Malika (d. 1978), took intense
pride in their sons and daughters. In spite of the formality
with which husband-wife relationships are portrayed to the
outside world by traditional Moroccans, the affection and
mutual trust of this particular marriage was pervasive. Our
experience of the Mansuri household shattered many of the

preconceptions we had assimilated from our readings on the Middle East. In 1978, not long after Lalla Malika's death, I returned to Boujad. Together with some of his children, the Hajj took me to see his wife's grave. One accepts God's will, so the Hajj never spoke of his grief. As one of his sons later said, he did not have to use words. I was too choked up to speak, so intense were my memories of the warmth with which we had been received over the years and the realization of what her loss meant for the Hajj. By then he had retired. His openness remained, but the elaborate, often joyous, hospitality of his household was now a past memory.

There is no easy answer to why Hajj 'Abd ar-Rahman chose to work with me. As one of his sons later said, his father never particularly liked Europeans and, as a speaker of only Arabic and *tashalḥīt*, he had limited means of communicating with them, in any case. Part of the answer lies, of course, in the common project of analyzing the Sharqawi papers, the importance of which we each understood in our different ways, but with a growing mutual respect for the questions and perceptions of the other. Our style of work and living also overlapped, at least in superficial respects. There was enough of the ascetic in me to dispense with ordinary periods of rest and eating to accomplish my self-imposed tasks. I soon learned that in addition to observing the Ramaḍān fast, 'Abd ar-Rahman fasted several days every month, a habit acquired from his father. Another consideration was that the qadi was engaged in identifiable scholarship in our common project. I think that he enjoyed such work as an end in itself. With me, even as a non-Muslim, he could at least temporarily pick up the threads of the world of learning he was abruptly compelled to leave when recalled by his elder brother to Bzu in 1935.

In more recent years I have had several opportunities to speak about my intended book with his children, now adults, and they have freely shared with me their thoughts about their father. As one of them observed, their father discussed his own youth and education with me in a detail that he did not seek to convey to his own children, although his relation with them was close, supportive, and affectionate. They are of a generation that has received a Western-style education in Moroccan government schools, in one case the palace school. For this generation, Quranic education has been little more than a preschool. Even the technical terms necessary to discuss the style of education their father received remain unfamiliar to them, as is the emphasis upon memorization of the word of God and related texts. In contrast, I was interested in the world of learning as 'Abd ar-Rahman had experienced it, and by trial and error found the questions to ask so that this world began to make sense.

A colleague, a psychoanalyst with anthropological training, suggests a complementary reason for the close ties which developed between 'Abd ar-Rahman and myself. For the qadi, I may have taken over the role of a younger brother, allowing him to recreate the supportive relationship which he had with his own elder brother, described in the next three chapters, and at the same time pick up his commitment to learning where he left off decades earlier. He could transmit to me, as he unconsciously felt he could not to his own children, his own values and sensibilities concerning Islamic learning. I listened and judged, but also appreciated.

Each time I returned to Morocco in the 1970s, Hajj 'Abd ar-Rahman asked if my wife and I had children yet. Just before my wife and I adopted our first child in 1978, he said to me: "It doesn't matter. Books are the children of a man of learning." My books have decidedly taken a form other than the preferred ones of the "sciences" ('ulūm; sing. 'ilm) of his tradition of origin. But his tradition of learning has allowed him to find at least partial homologies in other traditions and to respect them. As I learned through our discussions of religious studies and the Yusufiya milieu, learning how to ask questions and make sense of other traditions of knowledge was in itself a component of the mosque-university tradition.

TWO

Beginnings

The ancient towne of Bzo is built vpon a high hill . . .
The townesmen are honest people, exercising merchan-
dize, and going decently apparelled: To them which in-
habit the deserts they carie cloth, oile, and leather. Their
mountaines abound with oliues, corne, and all kinde of
fruits: and of their grapes they make euery yeere most
excellent and sweete raisins. Figs they haue great plentie:
and their walnut-trees are so high, that a puttocke may
securely builde his nest vpon the tops: for it is impossible
for any man to climbe vp. On each side of the way which
leadeth from hence to the riuer Guadelhabid there are
most pleasant and beautiful gardens. My selfe (I remember) was here present when their oranges, figs, and other
fruits were growen to ripenes.
—Leo Africanus 1896 (orig. 1526): II, 304

BZU AND ITS REGION

'Abd ar-Rahman's home from his birth until 1957 does not
entirely live up to the rhapsodic description of Leo Africanus. For a piedmont (*dīr*) village in the Marrakesh hinterland, Bzu nevertheless has a pleasant, modestly prosperous
appearance in sharp contrast to the scorched villages of the
Srāghna plain to its immediate south. Bzu is actually a cluster
of juxtaposed hamlets on adjacent hills, located about ten
kilometers south of the main highway that connects it with
Marrakesh, the imperial capital and commercial entrepôt for
Morocco's south. Travel to the main highway was by mule
until the 1930s. Now busses leave directly from Bzu's marketplace for Marrakesh, 130 kilometers and by bus three
hours away, and Qal'at Srāghna, a dusty provincial capital

50 kilometers to the west. Sraghna's expansion since the mid-1960s is linked to the massive growth of agribusiness in its immediate hinterland. Its growth sharply differs from the relative decline of piedmont villages such as Bzu, located in regions marginally suitable for modern agricultural techniques.

Until the late 1960s, many cultivators near Bzu still used camels and mules to draw irrigation water, although today small motor pumps have finally replaced most animal power. The Bzu region is given over to the herding of sheep and goats, and to orchard cultivation, principally of olives, oranges, and figs, and secondarily pomegranates and other fruits. The countryside is dry and barren for most of the year except for the irrigated orchards, although wheat and barley are grown in years when rainfall is sufficient.

Rainfall averages 400 millimeters (16 inches) annually, concentrated mostly in the months of November through April, although droughts regularly recur. Those of 1936 and 1945 enabled major local notables vastly to expand their personal holdings at the expense of tribesmen with small plots, many of whom became reluctant sharecroppers. Until the late 1960s, when money sent home by emigrant workers began to alleviate the poverty of some families, there was a substantial economic gap between a few prosperous notables and the large number of sharecroppers and tenants. In Bzu in 1969, it was still common to see sharecroppers and tenants kiss the hands of local notables, a greeting practiced further north only by sons to their fathers as an act of deference and respect. Only a few sullen, "progressive" schoolteachers posted from elsewhere in Morocco ostentatiously used the less inegalitarian handshake. A few tribesmen went so far as to kiss feet, although local notables were embarrassed by this gesture in the presence of foreign visitors.

Bzu still had a limited importance as a regional market until the late 1940s for nearby tribes of the High Atlas region and those of the plains. Olive oil is processed locally and shipped to other regions, and most of the oranges find their way through auction to markets in Casablanca and Marrakesh.

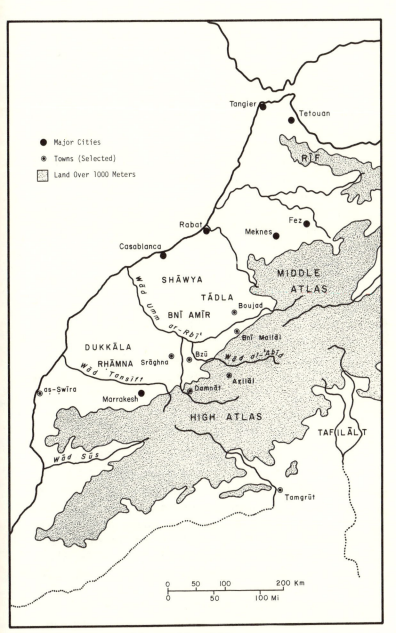

MAP 1. Map of Morocco.

Until the early 1960s, one of the hamlets of Bzu was a Jewish settlement. Its economic activities included itinerant trade with outlying villages, tailoring, shoemaking, blacksmithing, and carpentry, activities now continued by former Muslim apprentices. The manufacture of large clay jars is still a local speciality, although Bzu is best known for its distinctive silk tunics (jallabas) with alternating black and white stripes, a speciality of the artisans of the region. Sultan Mulay Hasan I (r. 1873-1894) was so impressed by these tunics that he attached Bzu weavers to his entourage. The silk was locally spun until the late nineteenth century, when higher-quality thread imported from Europe undercut its production. Bzu jallabas continued to be woven locally through the 1920s (Pascon 1977: 398, 414); their manufacture now survives with two old couples living inside the palace compound in Rabat, who weave them exclusively for the royal family. Women in Bzu still weave and sell for the local market the distinctive ḥayk Bzīwī, a brightly colored blanket worn as an outer garment by rural women.

Inhabitants of the region nearly all speak tashalhit, the Berber language of the High Atlas mountains, although by the 1920s many of the men and some of the women were already fluent in Arabic. By the early 1970s only older women and a few men in outlying settlements were unable to converse in Arabic.

Bzu's economic and political ties with the rest of Morocco are shifting and complex. Since at least the late eighteenth century, the region has been firmly under Makhzan control (Tawfīq 1983). Beginning with the reign of Mulay Hasan I, the region was subject to a qaid appointed by the sultan, who resided in the High Atlas town of Damnāt. Nonetheless, government presence in the region remained modest. Until almost the very end of the French protectorate (1912-1956), the religious court was held in the house of the qadi, 'Abd ar-Rahman's elder brother, who was also one of the major landowners. Today there is a small administrative center with a deputy qaid, a school, a court, and a small medical dispensary next to the marketplace.

Until the late 1960s these buildings and a few small shops next to the market were almost the only ones of outwardly modern construction. Most of the houses were adobe and mud brick. Today there are many cement houses, constructed with remittances from workers in France and other European countries. Although it is increasingly difficult to secure work in Europe and many "guest workers"—called "vacationers" (*fakāns*) in local Arabic because they return to Morocco only for their annual leave—have now permanently returned to Morocco, the economic impact of remittances and exposure to life elsewhere has mitigated the more extreme expressions of status inequality in the region. By the 1980s, the kissing of hands of notables was a rapidly dying tradition, although the marks of economic inequality remain strong.

THE FAMILY MILIEU: ORIGINS

The Arabic literary form of the tarjama encompasses the two genres of biography and autobiography in contemporary Western literature. Knowing the highly stylized conventions of the tarjama and being able to use them to describe one's own life or the lives of others is a skill known to every man of learning. For this reason, asking a man of learning for his tarjama acknowledges his status and provides a convenient port of entry to comprehending his social world.

A tarjama is always written in the third person, even if the life described is one's own. Its components include a genealogy, an account of formal education beginning with memorization of the Quran, specific books and subjects studied, poetry, aphorisms and other contributions to learning, sons taught by the father, and the names of important pupils. Specific dates are provided whenever possible, for the ability to date events itself distinguishes the traditionally educated from the unlearned.

The tarjama represents reality in a highly stylized manner.

Any element of the tarjama can be elaborated through relevant anecdotes or citations for which the exact provenance is specified. The words uttered are reported as if they were verbatim. Quotation marks are not used, and the stylistic tag, "he said to him" (*qāl lū*) does not clearly distinguish between actual speech and paraphrase. The tarjama asserts a literal representation of words and deeds based upon credible sources.

Although the tarjama is a necessary point of departure in describing the life of a man of learning, its stylistic conventions render it incomplete. No women are mentioned in it, so the family and household context in which early learning occurs is difficult to comprehend. Likewise, although teachers are mentioned, peer learning does not form part of the convention of the tarjama and is passed over in silence, as are politics and economic transactions, subjects that occupy a not insignificant amount of time for many men of learning.

Tarjamas of Moroccan men of learning in the late nineteenth and early twentieth centuries suggest the pervasive importance of close relatives in shaping their attitude toward learning. Mukhtār as-Sūsī's *al-Ma'sūl* (1961), a compendium of such biographies for Morocco's Sūs region, famous for its scholars, indicates that men of learning most often come from households in which the father or another close relative is already literate and takes an active role in teaching Quranic recitation or encouraging its study (e.g., as-Susi 1961: IX, 35-36, 101, 168).

Manṣūr bin Aḥmad (d. 1946), 'Abd ar-Rahman's father, was closely involved in the early education of his sons. Mansur had three sons and a daughter by Fāṭima, his first wife and 'Abd ar-Rahman's mother. Mansur divorced Fatima when 'Abd ar-Rahman was about five years old, and she left Bzu to return to her father. The eldest son was Ahmad (1312/1894-1895—1975), followed in order of birth by 'Abd ar-Rahman (1330/1912-), Zahra (c. 1914-1344/1925), and Muhammad (c. 1915-1978). He also had three sons and three daughters from Baṭūl, his second wife. The daughters by both marriages remained illiterate, but all his sons by the first marriage studied at the Yusufiya, and two of them completed their studies with distinction, as did two of the three sons by his second marriage.[1] Batul's youngest son, 'Abd al-Kabīr, born in the mid-1930s, was the only one not to receive a traditional education. Traditional religious studies had declined by the time he was ready for school, so he entered a government school instead. Soon after independence in 1956 he became a primary school teacher.

'Abd ar-Rahman knows little of his father's origins. Mansur rarely spoke of the subject to his children. Hence what they know of their father derives largely from what they observed and later discovered for themselves. Unlike many Moroccans, 'Abd ar-Rahman says he also knows little of his maternal relatives, although a maternal uncle taught him part of the Quran and was influential in his early education. His claim to know little of them, like the claim that he never visited his mother after her divorce because of the difficulty of travel, may relate more to the tensions present in the household of his youth than to actual circumstances.

Some religious figures and men of learning assert long genealogies linking them to famous ancestors or the house of the Prophet (Eickelman 1976: 183-210). 'Abd ar-Rahman's legal studies and sense of self led him to claim descent only from ancestors he could verify. Thus his "chain" of descent stopped at the level of his paternal grandfather. For 'Abd ar-Rahman, it is more important for a man of learning to assert only verifiable descent than to speculate over possible ante-

---

[1] 'Abd al-Ḥayy, the eldest son by this marriage, began his studies in Marrakesh in the early 1930s, not at the Yusufiya, but at the Darqāwī zawiya under the reformist shaykh, Mukhtār as-Sūsī (1900-1963). In 1935 as-Susi was exiled to his native Sus and the zawiya closed. A year later, 'Abd al-Hayy went to Fez, where, with the intervention of his father, who had excellent relations with the influential Shaykh 'Abd al-Hayy al-Kittani, he managed to enter the Qarawiyin. In 1949 he obtained a diploma from the Qarawiyin, then became a secretary in the Ministry of Justice in Rabat. After independence he was appointed successively as qadi in Damnat, as-Swira (1959), examining magistrate in Marrakesh (1962) and finally Qadi for Personal Affairs and Property in 1974, a post he held until his death.

TABLE I. THE DESCENDANTS OF MANSUR B. AHMAD OF BZU (d.1946)
(most dates are approximate)

Children	Children's Spouses, Grandchildren, and Great-Grandchildren in 1978

By his first wife, FATIMA B. AL-KABIR
(divorced 1917, d.1928)

Children	Children's Spouses, Grandchildren, and Great-Grandchildren in 1978
1. *Ahmad* (1895–1975), Yusufiya student (1913–1918), notary and scribe for French Native Affairs officers (1919–1925), qadi of Bzu (1925–1953), qaid and qadi of Ntifa (1956), qadi (1956–1957), member of Constitutional Council (1960), member of parliament (1963).	*First wife*: daughter of a Bzu shaykh (m.1920, d.1930s). *Children*: Muhammad al-Kabir (1926–). Yusufiya dropout; oversees father's estates. Married; childless. *Muhammad as-Saghir* (1939–). Qarawiyin dropout. Works with elder brother. Married a soldier's daughter, Bni Millal. Four sons, two daughters. *Second wife*: Daughter of protectorate qaid of Bzu (m.1935, d.1960s). *Children*: One daughter, Fatima, married to a court clerk.
2. *'Abd ar-Rahman* (1912–), Yusufiya student (1928–1935), deputy qadi of Bzu (1935–1953), qadi of Boujad (1957–1969), elsewhere (1969–1975). Pilgrimage to Mecca, 1960.	*Wife*: Lalla Malika (m.1941, d.1978). Sister of Ahmad's second wife. *Children*: *Hasan*, inspector of finance. Married, three children. Casablanca. *Mukhtar*, accountant. Married, two small children. *Habiba*, married. Husband is provincial director of education. Four children. *'Abd al-Ghani*, secondary school teacher, member of municipal council, Boujad. *al-Hajj*, student. *Yasin*, formerly student at Palace school, now in university, Rabat. *Fatima Zahra*, student. Three other children who died as infants, Bzu; two in Boujad.

TABLE 1 *(cont.)*

Children	Children's Spouses, Grandchildren, and Great-Grandchildren in 1978
3. *Muhammad* (1915–1978), Yusufiya dropout, notary.	*Wife*: Daughter of a local shaykh. Several small children.
4. *Zahra*, d.1925.	*Husband*: From Bzu. One son, a cupper (*ḥajjām*), two daughters.

By his second wife, BATUL BINT SALAH

1. *'Abd al-Hayy* (1922–1977), Yusufiya student to 1935, then Qarawiyin (1937–1949). Scribe, Ministry of Justice, Rabat (1949–1956), qadi in Damnat (1956–1959), as-Swira (1959–1962). Examining magistrate, Marrakesh (1962–1974), qadi (1974–1977). Pilgrimage in 1968.	*Wife*: From Bzu. *Children*: One daughter (1959–), English teacher, Marrakesh. Three sons; one is a merchant, two are students.
2. *'Abd al-'Aziz* (d.1936), had just begun studies at Yusufiya.	
3. *Mina* (d.1930s).	*Husband*: 'Umar, a fqih from Bzu. *Children*: A son, now teaching in Rabat. Two daughters; one died young, the other is married and living in Bzu.
4. *'Abd al-Kabir* (1935–), primary school teacher, near Bni Mallal.	*Wife*: Unknown. *Children*: Several.
5. *'Aysha*	*Husband*: From Bzu. *Children*: One daughter, Bzu.
6. *Fatima*	*Husband*: Brother of a qadi. *Children*: Unknown.

cedents, even when suggested by other men of learning. He recalled three childhood incidents that fed his curiosity as to his father's origins. On one occasion, a descendant of the Prophet (shrīf; pl. shurfā) visited his father and asked him to visit his other shrif relations in Ait Shitāshin, a tribe in the High Atlas mountains. Mansur declined the invitation. 'Abd ar-Rahman explained that such a journey would have been extremely arduous in the early part of this century. There were still no roads into the High Atlas mountains, and the region was outside the sphere of effective colonial control.

On another occasion, tribesmen claiming to be "close" (qrīb) to his father visited Bzu.[2] Pointing to Ahmad, they said that one day he would become a great man. The implication of this account is that the visitors, by prescient allusion to Ahmad's future success, may have claimed powers sometimes attributed to descendants of the Prophet. If they were shurfa and their claims of "closeness" with Mansur were valid, then of course Mansur could also claim descent from Muhammad. Finally, in the 1940s, by which time the Mansuris had long been established as prominent rural notables, a scholar from Marrakesh visited them on the pretext that he had managed to trace their lineage back to the Prophet. His intent was to be rewarded financially for the effort, which the Mansuri brothers declined to do although he was honored as a guest. 'Abd ar-Rahman cautioned me to regard these incidents as "just so" stories.

How Mansur settled in Bzu and established ties in the region remains unclear. Mansur told his sons that he came from Tagharāt, a Berber village "above" Damnat in the High Atlas mountains. Neither 'Abd ar-Rahman nor his elder brother ever visited the village. However, Mansur once told Ahmad that a major land dispute broke out between two tribal groups in Tagharat. Mansur's father, Ahmad, had been warned to come down to Bzu to avoid being attacked. He ignored the

[2] See Eickelman (1976: 96-99) for an account of the variable ways in which social ties are elaborated and expressed in Morocco.

warning, so one night four marauders broke into his house, killing him and plundering his belongings. Mansur managed to escape to Bzu, together with his son Ahmad, then barely forty days old, hidden in his tunic. The incident is indirectly datable. In Ahmad's tarjama, written in 1962 at the request of a schoolteacher from another region of Morocco assigned to Bzu, he gives the year of his birth as 1312/1894-1895. This incident may have been another compelling reason that Mansur declined to return to his village of origin later in his life.

Marriages among rural notables in the first part of this century were strategically calculated political events. One of Mansur's sisters married a rural shaykh of the Bzu region whose family had held the shaykhship since the mid-nineteenth century. Mansur's first wife and 'Abd ar-Rahman's mother, Fatima, was daughter of a rural shaykh from Tamānnt, a village about fifteen kilometers distant from Bzu on a difficult mountain path. These marriages suggest that Mansur had some sort of claim to notable status and a specific link to the Bzu region prior to his sudden flight from Tagharat. Yet the matter remains unclear. His younger sisters all married Quranic teachers or literate men—the term *fqīh* covers both— in the Bzu region, one of whom was a messenger for Sultan Mulay Hasan I. Mansur's only brother, Muhammad, described by 'Abd ar-Rahman as "tough and harsh" in temperament, joined the Spanish army in the Rif in the 1920s, served with Franco's forces in the Spanish Civil War, and remained in the Spanish army until 1950, when he retired to Bzu and died there a few years later. Muhammad claimed that his wife, from Morocco's Spanish zone, was a descendant of the prophet (*shrīfa*), another assertion regarded as unverifiable by 'Abd ar-Rahman.

More certain is the fact that by the time of 'Abd ar-Rahman's birth in 1330/1912, Mansur had become a minor landowner in the region and was respected throughout the region for his stern piety. Because of his dual reputation for piety and hospitality, Mansur often entertained men of learning and religious figures as they passed through Bzu. He was an adherent of the Kittāniya religious order (ṭarīqa). He regularly set aside a few days each month for fasts supplemental to that incumbent upon all Muslims in the month of Ramadan, made a personal prayer (da'wa) before every meal and, when not engaged in conversation, moved his lips in silent recitation of the Quran. These practices are still common among pious Moroccans, but Mansur adopted other practices now deemed religiously questionable. Every afternoon, as he sat in the courtyard of his house in Tagūnnt, the hilltop hamlet in Bzu where his house was located, he struck a sharp rock rhythmically against his head and forearms, often drawing blood. During 'Abd ar-Rahman's youth, this was a practice common to members of the Kittani order.

From today's vantage point, Mansur's personal piety may appear part of a "traditional" practical religion with no certain temporal dimension. At least for the Bzu region, the Kittani practice of self-mortification was an early twentieth-century innovation. Self-mortification was practiced by other religious orders such as the Ḥaddāwa (Brunel 1955) and the Ḥamādsha (Crapanzano 1973), but not by religious orders such as the Kittaniya, which attracted notables as adherents. Mansur's style of religiosity marked an era, for none of his sons joined the Kittaniya or adopted any of the practices identified with religious orders. Although the sons avoided direct confrontation with their father, they flatly considered self-mortification to be beyond the pale of Islamic practice. Their generation was one heavily influenced by reformist Islam, which considered religious orders and their practices as distortions of Islam. Nonetheless, the Mansuri brothers were their father's sons in other respects. From their youth they performed supplemental fasts, recited invocations before meals, and moved their lips in recitation of the Quran when not engaged in conversation.

Mansur's piety gave him a quasi-maraboutic status among the tribesmen of the region. He often was called upon to mediate local disputes. From 1916 until his death from typhus in 1946 he was prayer-leader (imām) at the principal mosque in Bzu, and until the French reformed the notarial system in the early 1920s he served as notary. He wrote whatever documents tribesmen requested of him in the marketplace or wherever he happened to be. As was the practice prior to the French reforms, he kept no copy or register of documents that he prepared, nor did he ask a fee. If grateful tribesmen gave him money, he disbursed it as alms to children and the poor at the market. Once French reforms were implemented, the documents he prepared were no longer regarded as legally valid; the French never granted him notarial status. Nonetheless, tribesmen unaware of the fact continued to seek his services until his death. Ahmad, after he became qadi of Bzu in 1344/1925, quietly avoided confrontation with his father by redoing without payment his father's documents in acceptable form. Mansur never learned of his son's emendations. To his death, he thought that he had successfully avoided the strictures placed upon him by French rule.

Two incidents indicate Mansur's stature in the region and also suggest the nuances of successful adjustment to colonial rule. In 1338/1919 Ahmad was engaged by the French to make an inventory of all pious endowment (*aḥbās*) lands in the Ntifa region, of which Bzu formed a part. In that same year the French began to implement the rural tax (*tartīb*). Since this was a non-Islamic tax, tribesmen resisted paying in many regions. Like many other educated persons in rural Morocco, Ahmad was obliged by the French to cooperate with the qaids and shaykhs, many of whom were illiterate, in establishing the system. In Bzu the tax was at first paid in kind. To avoid resistance to its payment, Ahmad arranged for his father's house to be used as a collection point for the produce. As a consequence, resistance to imposition of the new tax was minimal because most tribesmen assumed that they were making a religiously sanctioned tithe (*'ushūr*).

The second incident occurred in 1925. The government-appointed shaykhs and headmen (*mqaddim*s) of the Bzu region, together with Mansur, were called to a meeting at the weekly Bzu market with the new qaid of Ntifa, Sī Muḥammad

49

bin 'Abd Allāh ash-Shtīwī. The qaid, an illiterate, raised publicly the issue of a contested property title (*rasm*) that Mansur had prepared. It was common knowledge that documents prepared by him were invalid. The qaid looked briefly at the document, which he pretended to read, then handed it back to Mansur, saying that it was improperly executed. Mansur bluntly asked the qaid: "And just what do you know of Islamic law? Absolutely nothing." The qaid slapped Mansur and curtly ordered him to leave the assembly. Mansur did, but immediately sent a messenger to his eldest son with a letter, asking him to return immediately to Bzu. In the meantime, friends of the qaid informed him that Mansur and his elder son were the two most influential men in Bzu, and that the incident might spark a local uprising that would call the qaid's ability to govern into doubt. Once Ahmad returned to Bzu—he had been working elsewhere as a scribe (then an influential post) for a French Native Affairs officer—he arranged an uneasy truce (*sulḥ*) between the qaid and his father. From that time on, the qaid sought to better his relations with the Mansuri family. The qaid supported appointing Ahmad as overseer (*nāḍir*) of pious endowments that same year, and his appointment as qadi a few months later.

A Qadi's Childhood

The first step in acquiring an Islamic education in Morocco is memorization of the Quran and its proper recitation. 'Abd ar-Rahman first entered the mosque-school (*msīd*), at the age of four, just before his mother left the household, and became a "memorizer" (*ḥāfiḍ*) around 1924. Mansur was as stern with his sons in disciplining them to memorize the word of God as he was with himself. 'Abd ar-Rahman recalled:

> What I remember most of my childhood is the cane. When we were young, my brothers and I were beaten three times daily by my father: morning, noon, and night. Each night

he required us to stand before him and recite five *ḥizb*s of the Quran.[3] Other children were only expected to recite one. If we made a mistake, then we would be beaten again.

At no time throughout our discussions did 'Abd ar-Rahman indicate resentment over such beatings. On the contrary, he says that the beatings were a sign of his father's concern for him and his other brothers. As he emphasizes, his father never beat him in anger. Another Moroccan educated in this tradition has shown me the scars encircling his neck from where his father regularly twisted his flesh whenever he made a mistake in recitation. In this case as well, the father's actions were described as proper concern for conveying the word of God to the son, not as cruelty.[4]

The patterns of domestic authority in the households in which 'Abd ar-Rahman matured are central to his early memories. As was common with other families of notables, the households in which he grew up—there were several—each consisted of several conjugal couples and their children. Frequent shifts in the membership of these households were not uncommon.

When 'Abd ar-Rahman was five, Mansur took a second wife, Batul. This radically altered the household, for Fatima was adamantly opposed to the second marriage and returned to

[3] For recitational purposes, the Quran is divided into sixty sections (hizbs) of approximately equal length.

[4] The Senegalese novelist Cheikh Hamidou Kane (1963: 3-38) provides the only account of which I am aware that manages to convey the mixture of pious respect for exact recitation of the word of God and affection for their students associated with the severity of Quranic teachers toward their students. In one of many tarjamas presented by as-Susi (1961: IX, 35), a father obliged his son constantly to accompany him and to hold his slate, on which were written the Quranic passages to be memorized, before him. If his attention wandered and he was within reach of his father's stick he would be beaten. If he was further away his father threw small stones. In this fashion the student memorized the Quran in six different recitational forms.

her father's house in Tamannt. She took her daughter, Zahra, with her, but was compelled to leave her sons behind. Soon afterward she was divorced. 'Abd ar-Rahman saw her only once more before she died in the late 1920s.

His mother's departure was a significant loss. In common with other educated Moroccans of his generation, 'Abd ar-Rahman did not dwell upon his "inner" feelings or elaborate upon the psychological consequences of separation from his mother. Even in speaking of women we had radically departed from the conventions of biography. Yet his choice of recollections suggests a sense of profound loss. In practical terms, 'Abd ar-Rahman and his younger brother (Ahmad had already left Bzu to pursue studies in Marrakesh) were left in a household with a young stepmother, unsure of her status because she was still without children of her own. She was hostile toward the children of Mansur's first marriage from the start. Her attitude did not soften after she bore her own children, who in birth order were 'Abd al-Ḥāyy (1922-1977). 'Abd al-'Azīz (d. 1936), Mīna (d. 1930s), 'Abd al-Kabir (c. 1935-), 'Āysha and Fāṭima. 'Abd ar-Rahman remembers sitting in the courtyard when his stepmother came up behind him with a bucket of filthy washing-water which she poured over his head. He says that such incidents were common. Even if his recollection of this incident is highly selective, it probably conveys accurately how he felt at this time in his life. Mansur continued his strict supervision of his sons' Quranic studies, but left household matters to his second wife.

A comparison with the seventeenth-century Moroccan scholar, Sidi al-Hasan al-Yusi, also born in a rural milieu, serves to place 'Abd ar-Rahman's childhood trauma in perspective. Berque (1958: 10) comments that the death of al-Yusi's mother in his early childhood was a shock that "emptied the home and discolored the universe," with the consequence that al-Yusi intellectualized his loss and took refuge in his studies.

Given the vicissitudes of natural circumstances and the facility with which divorce can be accomplished, many Moroccans experience the loss of a parent in childhood.[5] A mitigating factor, much less present in situations in which nuclear families are separately housed, is that several relatives often share responsibilities for raising children. This was the case for 'Abd ar-Rahman. After his mother's divorce, 'Abd ar-Rahman often stayed for weeks on end at the nearby house of a maternal uncle, Muḥammad bin al-Kabīr Abarrāḥ, who was also one of his Quranic teachers. Perhaps indirectly recognizing the tense situation in his own household, Mansur intermittently gave small gratuities to this uncle until his death in the early 1920s, in recognition of his role in 'Abd ar-Rahman's education and upbringing. 'Abd ar-Rahman's elder brother later took over this role.

In 1918, when Ahmad returned temporarily to Bzu and resided in his father's house, his presence and forceful personality restrained Batul's cruelty. 'Abd ar-Rahman says that she was afraid of him. When Ahmad returned from Marrakesh, Mansur built a small mosque within the compound of his house. There 'Abd ar-Rahman continued his memorization alongside his younger half-brothers, 'Abd al-'Aziz and 'Abd al-Hayy.

His Brother's Footsteps

Ahmad's career framed that of 'Abd ar-Rahman. Not only did 'Abd ar-Rahman admire his elder brother; his elder brother's decisive influence in local politics defined his practical possibilities until the end of the colonial era.

Although Ahmad was only eight years older than 'Abd ar-Rahman, he belonged to a generation of men of learning who came to maturity just as the machinery of the protectorate was set into place. Some opportunistically realized the possibilities open to them through collaboration. Others, al-

---

[5] Maher (1974: 193-198) reports that divorces as a percentage of marriages in the Middle Atlas region which she studied in the 1960s was 52 percent in villages and 38 percent in towns. Roughly comparable figures are provided by Geertz, Geertz, and Rosen (1979: 386-391).

though displeased with French rule, saw no realistic alternative to working within the system being established by the
French. Only a few chose openly to resist the French (see
Hammoudi 1981). Ahmad, a devout Muslim and courageous
in his own right—the French awarded him a medal—was a
realist.

Ahmad completed memorizing the Quran in 1328/1911.
Soon afterward he left Bzu to study with Muḥammad bin ʻAlī
al-Mshābbkī, a scholar who taught religious studies to a fluctuating number of ten to twenty Berber-speaking students in
a tent school at Dawwār Mshabbak, located twelve kilometers
south of Bzu. ʻAbd ar-Rahman was to attend this same school
a decade later. Such tent schools were especially common
among Berber scholars, who had first to acquire sufficient skill
in Arabic in order later to pursue studies at such centers of
higher learning as the Yusufiya. The school at Dawwar
Mshabbak was sophisticated enough that in addition to teaching the religious sciences, one of its teachers during Ahmad's
stay there also taught elementary arithmetic, at the time a
curricular innovation.[6]

In 1331/1913, Ahmad left the Bzu region for the Yusufiya,
where he remained until 1336/1918. Upon his return to Bzu
in that year, he set up a school (madrasa) of his own in his
father's house, where he fed and clothed a fluctuating number
of six to twelve religious students (ṭulba; s. ṭalib), characterized by ʻAbd ar-Rahman as mostly impecunious blacks from
southern Morocco.

In 1338/1919 Ahmad again left Bzu under orders to assist
the French Native Affairs officer responsible for Ntifa. He
also received a military medal that year from the French, the

---

[6] The math taught was similar to our own conception of the subject. This
specification is needed because there was another form of mathematics prevalent in traditional learning in the Marrakesh region, al-ḥisāb al-ḥimārī, in
which all basic mathematical functions were performed, but in a manner
more cumbersome than that taught in European schools. According to Muhammad Aafif (personal communication, 1984), it was still taught at zawiya
Sīdī Zwayn, about 30 kilometers west of Marrakesh, in the 1950s.

Ouissam al-Harb, a fact omitted from his 1962 tarjama, for his aid in pacifying the Ait 'Tāb (Ait Attab), a large tribe near Azilāl. He also became a notary in 1919, at the time a significant post, especially for a youth of twenty-four. As miniscule as the rural administrative apparatus that was elaborated in the first years of the colonial era retrospectively appears, it constituted a major expansion over precolonial local administration. Many of the Moroccans to participate in colonial administration from the outset were quickly promoted to posts that secured their prominence as regional notables in the years to come. Ahmad bin Mansur was one of them.

In 1920 Ahmad returned once again to Bzu, already a prominent local notable despite his youth. Although he at first lived once again in his father's house, he was aware of the serious potential for conflict. Ahmad had begun to eclipse his father in importance, because Mansur was unsuccessful in adapting to the changed circumstances of colonial administration. Although Mansur continued to be highly respected, an increasing stream of visitors came primarily to see Ahmad. Recognizing the delicacy of the situation, Ahmad began construction of his own house, some 800 meters away from that of his father's. It was completed in 1923. From that time on, 'Abd ar-Rahman spent most of his time at his brother's house.

In 1343/1924-1925, Ahmad was called away again by the French to become secretary to the French officer in Azilal assigned to the Ait 'Tab. He at first refused, but was obliged to accept the assignment for a year. He took 'Abd ar-Rahman along with him. In the third-person usage characteristic of tarjamas, one of which 'Abd ar-Rahman prepared at my request in 1976, he records that his brother placed him in the care of a renowned teacher among the Ait 'Tab, "one of God's people" (*min ahl Allāh*), who supervised his studies in a mosque-school "which attracted a large number of students. [The teacher] slept little in the night; instead, he praised God. This teacher favored the fqih 'Abd ar-Rahman [over other students] to accompany him in the dawn prayers." Although

'Abd ar-Rahman had not yet completed memorization of the Quran, he began parallel memorization of the *Ajārūmīya*, a compact grammar in verse.[7] He also began memorizing the *Alfīya* of Ibn Mālik (d. 672/1274). This book is a grammar in one thousand rhymed verses judged by Berque (1949: 75) to be so compact as to be obscure and often unintelligible. Both these treatises were recognized as beginner's texts (*al-mabādi'*), commonly the first books after the Quran to be memorized by students (as-Susi 1961: IX, 101). Since these texts and certain others were memorized by all educated men, there was no ambiguity in the common practice of referring to them by title only. Although these two books are not memorized with the same care as the Quran, rural men of learning often lace verses from them into their conversations and vie with one another to recall their verses.

From 1925 until early 1927, 'Abd ar-Rahman returned to Bzu, where he studied alongside his half-brothers in his father's house. He continued memorization of the Quran, the *Ajarumiya*, and the *Alfīya*, and in addition began memorization of Ibn 'Asīm's (d. 1426) *Tuhfat al-Ḥukkām*, a 104-chapter handbook of practical jurisprudence with 1,679 verses. He also was introduced to the *Mukhtaṣar* of Khalīl ibn Isḥāq (d. 1378), the staple summary of the Mālikī school of jurisprudence in Morocco and cornerstone to the mnemonic culture of Moroccan men of learning. His activities were confined to memorizing these texts. Only later, as we shall see in the next chapter, did he acquire an understanding of what they meant.

---

[7] Written by Abū 'Abd Allāh Sīdī Muḥammad ibn Da'ūd as-Sanhājī ("Ibn Ajarrum") (d. 726/1324).

THREE

The Education of a Qadi: The Quranic Presence

ISLAMIC KNOWLEDGE IN MOROCCO

Why should some children spend years memorizing the Quran? The cultural idea of religious knowledge has remained remarkably constant over time throughout the regions of Islamic influence. Writing specifically of medieval Islamic civilization, Marshall Hodgson states that education was "commonly conceived as the teaching of fixed and memorizable statements and formulas which could be learned *without any process of thinking as such*" (Hodgson 1974: 438; emphasis added). The last phrase raises the crucial issue of the meaning of "understanding" associated with such a concept of knowledge. The "static and finite sum of statements" (ibid.) conveyed by education constitutes the religious sciences, the totality of knowledge and technique necessary in principle for a Muslim to lead the fullest possible religious life. They also constitute the most culturally valued knowledge (cf. Rosenthal 1970). The paradigm of all such knowledge is the Quran, considered literally to be the word of God; in Morocco its accurate memorization in one or more of the seven conventional recitational forms is the first step in mastering the religious sciences through "mnemonic possession" (*malakat al-ḥifḍ*).[1] The memorization of key texts just as the Quran is

---

[1] This is the contextual meaning of the term among contemporary Moroccan men of learning. Its meaning differs in other sociohistorical contexts. For instance, in psychological treatises of the ʿAbbāsid period the term implies "the faculty of memory." I am grateful to Roy Mottahedeh for pointing out this earlier usage.

memorized is also the starting point for the mastery of the religious sciences. To facilitate this task, most of the standard treatises used by Moroccan men of learning are written in rhymed verse.

Historians and sociologists have tended to take at face value the ideological claim in Islam of the fixed nature of religious knowledge. Consequently, not much attention has been given to a more critical analysis of how such a system of knowledge is affected by its mode of transmission and its linkages with other aspects of society. Thus, educated Muslims consider all bodies of knowledge that elucidate the "high words" (al-klām (al-'ālī) of the Quran and the traditions of the Prophet to comprise the religious sciences. Normatively speaking, the emphasis in transmitting this knowledge is conservational, especially in Morocco. Even Ibn Khaldūn (d. 1406) noted that the role of memory was stressed more in Morocco than elsewhere in the Islamic Middle East. It took sixteen years to acquire sufficient mastery of texts to teach on one's own in Morocco, owing to the necessity of memorization, but only five in Tunis (Ibn Khaldun 1967: II, 430-431). Given this emphasis, it is not surprising that contemporary Muslim and European scholars have expressed the most extreme opinions about Moroccan traditional education. Writing with a first-hand knowledge of the Qarawiyin of sixty years ago, a distinguished French historian and Arabist noted the "astonishing" (to a European) domestication of the memory involved in Islamic higher education. He claimed that it deadened the student's sense of inquiry to the point that the knowledge and comportment of twentieth-century men of learning could be assumed "without fear of anachronism" to be exact replicas of their predecessors of four centuries earlier (Lévi-Provençal 1922: 11). More recently, a Western scholar has written of the "stifling dullness" of Islamic education (L. C. Brown 1972: 71) and another, indicating perhaps an impatience with the unfamiliar principles upon which traditional Islamic education is based, claims that it "defies all [sic] pedagogical technique" (Berque 1974: 167). Islamic education fares no better in the hands of Western-educated Muslims, who write of it as a "purely mechanical, monotonous form of study" (Zerdoumi 1970: 196; also Hussein 1948).

Such common assumptions effectively mask the variety of Islamic educations—I deliberately use the plural—in different cultural contexts and historical periods. In my own experience, men of learning in Oman have listened in astonishment and occasional disbelief when I have stated that their counterparts in Morocco and even village Quranic teachers know the Quran by heart. In Oman, its proper recitation suffices. Moroccan scholars, for their part, show an equal astonishment to learn that they have counterparts elsewhere in the Islamic world who do not possess the Quran and other basic texts by memory. In twentieth-century Iran, there is much more formal dialogue between teachers and students as an ordinary component of higher education than is the case for Morocco, where such exchanges occurred principally in peer learning and private discussions. The presumption that Islamic learning in Morocco was merely a decayed form of the formal disputanda of *some* versions of "classical" and contemporary Islamic education is to neglect the diversity of this vital and complex tradition and favor description of those aspects of it, especially formal dialogue, that are more immediately appreciated by contemporary Western scholarship (Fischer 1980b; 1982; Makdisi 1981).

THE SOCIAL CONTEXT OF RELIGIOUS LEARNING

Sixty years ago, literacy in rural Morocco necessarily implied religious schooling, although schooling did not necessarily imply literacy. The first years of study consisted of memorizing and reciting the Quran; only at later stages did more advanced students learn to read and write, and then usually outside the context of the mosque school. Contemporary literacy is difficult to measure, let alone the literacy rates of earlier periods, but estimates are essential to indicate the scale of traditional education. For the 1920s and 1930s it appears reasonable to assume that a maximum of 4 percent of the adult male rural population was literate, allowing for regional variations, and perhaps 10-20 percent of the adult male urban population (Hart 1976: 183; H. Geertz 1979: 470-487; Brown 1976: 107). The rural estimate is appropriate to Bzu, where the uses for literacy outside of Quranic recitation included chiefly the ability of agricultural overseers to keep accounts for absentee landlords and write simple narratives of events in a rough and ready colloquial Arabic. Merchants and traders also had use for a limited literacy in corresponding with their suppliers elsewhere in Morocco. Quranic teachers sometimes wrote amulets and charms. A more complete literacy was required only by notaries, who had mastery of conventional legal formulas. Only a handful of persons possessed the self-consciously ornate literary style eventually mastered by 'Abd ar-Rahman. Arabic was an established second language in Bzu, Tashalhit was not used in written communications and records.

Religious learning was popularly respected. Some accounts of Morocco have postulated a sharp distinction between urban and rural religious practices. This is a difficult distinction to maintain. It has long been recognized that virtually every rural local community (*dawwār*) and traditional urban quarter is socially distinguished by a maraboutic shrine and ties with one or several maraboutic figures (Castries 1924; Jemma 1972; Eickelman 1976: 97, 102-103, 111-113). In the 1920s, as today, virtually every urban quarter and rural local community maintains a mosque school for which a teacher (fqih) was contracted on an annual basis to teach and to perform certain other religious services for the community.[2] Few of these teachers are supported by pious endowment funds in

---

[2] The only estimate of the number of these schools in any region is contained in a 1955 census conducted in Spanish Morocco: 3,392 for a population estimated at 917,000 (Valderrama 1956: map opposite p. 155; Noin 1970: I, 33). This means that there was a Quranic school for every 279 persons. Since none of the schools was supported by the government, it is reasonable to assume a similar proportion of schools to the population in the 1920s and 1930s.

urban contexts and almost none in rural ones. Their maintenance consequently indicates current and sustained community support. In rural contexts these schools often consisted
of no more than an ordinary tent or rural hut (*nwāla*), dis-
tinguishable from other dwellings only by a small flag run up
on a pole. The modest stipend for teachers was often partially
paid in kind, with even meals being prepared on a rotational
basis by members of the community.

Most Moroccan males and a fair number of females, at
least in towns, attended Quranic schools long enough to commit to memory a few passages of the Quran, but Quranic
schools were characterized by a high rate of attrition. Most
students left before they acquired literacy. Few remained the
six to eight years that were generally required to memorize
the entire Quran.[3]

The formal features of Quranic schools have been frequently described (e.g., Michaux-Bellaire 1911), although the
specific consequences of their form of pedagogy upon modes
of thought have only begun to be critically explored (see Wagner 1978, 1983; Wagner and Lotfi 1980). The Islamic emphasis upon memory is not unique, as has been implied by
some scholars. Elaborate mnemonic systems were developed
in classical Greece and Rome, which facilitated memorization
through the regular association of material with "memory
posts," visual images such as the columns of a building or
places at a banquet table (Yates 1966: 2-7). Accompanying
such techniques was the notion that mnemonic knowledge
was "purer" than that communicated through writing (Notopoulos 1938: 478). What is remarkable about the use of
memory in the context of Islamic education in Morocco is
not the performance of "prodigious" mnemonic feats, there-

[3] A 1974 study found that the average number of years spent in Quranic
school varied from close to two years in Marrakesh to a low of 0.33 years
in small mountain villages in the Middle Atlas (Wagner and Lotfi 1980: 241).
Most mosque schools today have taken on the role of preschools. Only in
remote rural areas do some students continue to remain for the time required
to memorize the entire Quran.

fore. Such feats were fully paralleled in Europe (Yates 1966). Rather, it is the insistence by former students that there were no devices to facilitate memorization. Although 'Abd ar-Rahman and most other former students can recall being able to visualize the shape of the letters upon their slates and even the circumstances associated with the memorization of particular Quranic verses and other texts, such potential mnemonic cues were not formally expressed, perhaps for the implicit reason that their use would associate extraneous images with the word of God and thus dilute its transmission. Although students deny the existence of mnemonic devices, Wagner (1978: 14) suggests that patterns of intonation and rhythm systematically serve as mnemonic markers.

A typical fqih had between fifteen and twenty students in his charge at any time, ranging in age from four to sixteen. No printed or manuscript copies of the Quran were used in the process of memorization. Each morning the fqih wrote the verses to be memorized on each student's wooden slate (*lūḥ*). The child then spent the rest of the day memorizing these verses by reciting them out loud, as well as systematically reciting verses that had been previously learned. Some students, such as 'Abd ar-Rahman, also laboriously traced the fqih's letters with a quill pen and an ink made locally of burned wool and charred sheep's horn.

Two features consistently associated with Islamic education are its rigorous discipline and the lack of explicit explanation of memorized material. Both of these features are congruent with the concept of essentially fixed knowledge which is at the base of Islamic education, at least in the Moroccan context, and the associated concept of "reason" (*'qāl*) prevalent in Moroccan society. Reason is popularly conceived as man's ability to discipline his nature in order to act in accord with the arbitrary code of conduct laid down by God and epitomized by such acts of communal obedience as the fast of Ramadan (see Eickelman 1976: 130-138). Thus a firm discipline in the course of learning the Quran is culturally regarded as an integral part of socialization. This underlying popular attitude toward learning is one of the reasons why it is inappropriate and misleading to see Islamic education as a "high tradition" grafted upon or independent of more popular implicit understandings of religion and society, as has been done by an earlier tradition of Orientalist and anthropological scholarship. In Moroccan towns and villages, the discipline of Quranic memorization is an integral part of learning to be human and Muslim.

When a father handed his son over to a fqih, he did so with the formulaic phrase that the child could be beaten as the fqih saw fit. Such punishments were considered necessary for accurate Quranic recitation of the word of God. Former students explained that the fqih (or the student's father, when he participated in supervising the process of memorization) was regarded as only the impersonal agency of the occasional punishments which, like the unchanging word of God itself, were merely transmitted by him. Moreover, as 'Abd ar-Rahman and others explained to me, students were told that any part of their bodies struck in the process of Quranic memorization would not burn in hell. (The same notion popularly applied to beatings which apprentices received from craftsmen [m'allmīn dyāl l-ḥarfa], including musicians, since music is popularly considered to be a craft [Schuyler 1979: 22-27]). In practice, students were slapped or whipped only when their attention flagged or when they repeated errors, although my impression from contemporary mosque schools is that the children of high-status fathers are struck much less frequently than other children.

Former students emphasized that throughout the long process of memorizing the Quran, they asked no questions concerning the meaning of verses, even among themselves, nor did it occur to them to do so. Their sole activity was memorizing proper Quranic recitation. It should be kept in mind that the grammar and vocabulary of the Quran are not immediately accessible to speakers of colloquial Arabic, and are even less so to students from Berber-speaking regions; 'Abd ar-Rahman, together with other former students, readily admitted to not comprehending what he was memorizing until fairly late in his studies (see also Hart 1976: 85; Waterbury 1972: 32). Only after 'Abd ar-Rahman had memorized the entire Quran did he hesitantly begin to converse in Arabic.

"Understanding" (*fahm*) was not measured by any ability explicitly to "explain" particular verses. Explanation was considered a science in itself to be acquired only through years in the advanced study of exegetical literature (*tafsīr*). Any informal attempt to explain meaning was considered blasphemy and simply did not occur. Instead, the measure of understanding was implicit and consisted in the ability to use particular Quranic verses in appropriate contexts. In the first few years of Quranic school, students recalled that they had little control over what they recited. They could not, for instance, recite specific chapters of the Quran if asked to do so, but had to begin by one of the sixty principal recitational sections. Firmer control was achieved as students accompanied their father, other relatives, and occasionally their fqih to social gatherings. On such occasions they heard adults incorporate Quranic verses into particular contexts and gradually acquired the ability to do so themselves, as well as to recite specific sections of the Quran without regard for the order in which they had memorized it. Thus the measure of understanding was the ability to make appropriate practical reference to the memorized text, just as originality was shown in working Quranic references into novel but appropriate contexts in conversation, in sermons, and on formal occasions. Knowledge and manipulation of secular oral poetry and proverbs in a parallel fashion is still a sign of good rhetorical style; the skill is not confined to religious learning (Geertz 1983: 112-113).

The high rate of attrition from Quranic schools supports the notion that mnemonic "possession" can be considered a form of cultural capital (Bourdieu 1973: 80). Aside from small customary gifts given by the parents of children to the fqih, education was free. Yet most students were compelled to drop out after a short period in order to contribute to the support of their families or because they failed to receive familial support, as did 'Abd ar-Rahman, for the arduous and imperfectly understood process of learning. In practice, memorization of the Quran was accomplished primarily by the children of relatively prosperous households or by those whose fathers or guardians were already literate. I say primarily, for education was still a means to social mobility, especially if a poor student managed to progress despite all obstacles through higher, post-Quranic education (cf. Green 1976: 218-221).

The notion of cultural capital implies more than the possession of the material resources to allow a child to spend six to eight years in the memorization of the Quran; it also implies a sustained adult discipline over the child. Many contemporary Western pedagogical concepts treat education as a separable institutional activity, but this idea is inappropriate to learning in the traditional Islamic context.[4] Students' fathers, elder brothers, other close relatives—including women in some cases (e.g., Waterbury 1972: 31-32)—and peers, especially at later stages of learning, were integrally involved in the learning process. These all provided contexts in which learning could continue. Even for urban students from wealthy families, formal education did not involve being systematically taught to read and write outside of the context of the Quran. Students acquired such skills, if at all, from relatives or older students apart from their studies in Quranic schools (Berque 1974: 167-168), just as they acquired a demonstrated understanding of the Quran through social situations in which Quranic verses and other memorized materials were used.

CARRIERS OF THE QURAN

A student became a "memorizer" (hafid) once he knew the entire Quran; its memorization gave him a special status in

---

[4] Such notions have also hampered the study of education in the West. For colonial America, see Bailyn (1960).

ordinary society.[5] During a child's memorization of the Quran, there was periodic public recognition of his progress. The Quran is composed of four quarters (*silka*s, lit. "threads") of fifteen hizbs each. After successful memorization of each quarter, a child's household was expected to offer a feast to which the teacher, neighbors, and others were invited. The largest celebration was reserved for memorization of the entire Quran, when the student would often be mounted on a gaily decorated mule (as was 'Abd ar-Rahman in 1927-1928) or horse for a celebratory progression through his town or village, accompanied by musicians, other students, and ululating women. Through the 1960s, such celebrations accompanied the awarding of diplomas in government schools. Now that education no longer guarantees employment or high status, the practice has fallen off.

In the precolonial era, fqihs, religious students, and Jewish traders, who themselves had a separate, distinctive role (Eickelman 1983), often were the only strangers who could travel in safety through tribal regions without making prior arrangements for protection. This special status was especially pronounced in rural and tribal milieus, where the Quranic teacher was often the only "stranger," in Simmel's (1964: 402-405) sense of the term, to live regularly in smaller villages and settlements.

Analysis of the role of rural Quranic teachers is especially useful in eliciting the popular significance of memorizing the Quran. Some teachers remained for decades with particular communities (e.g., Waterbury 1972: 32); in other cases, Quranic teachers changed locales at frequent intervals. Many fqihs lived from little more than small fees in cash and kind, sometimes supplemented by the weaving of jallabas (Hart 1976: 183-184). Poverty did not preclude respect for Quranic teachers as carriers of the Quran.

[5] Like other technical terms, *hafid* is subject to contextual variation. For 'Abd ar-Rahman and other educated Moroccans, the term is sparingly applied only to the most outstanding scholars of any generation. In popular usage, the term refers to anyone who has memorized the Quran.

Simmel's concept of the "stranger" is useful in comprehending the Quranic teacher's position in rural communities. As a "stranger,"the fqih "has not belonged to [local society] from the beginning" and "he imports qualities into it, which do not and cannot stem from the group itself" (Simmel 1964: 402). The fqih is "objective" in that he is not "radically committed" to the community, but his objectivity, to continue to apply Simmel's analysis, "does not simply involve passivity and detachment; it is a particular structure composed of distance and nearness, indifference and involvement." As a stranger, the fqih has only more general and abstract qualities in common with members of the community in which he participates. "He is near and far *at the same time*" (Simmel 1964: 406-407), and is a concrete symbol of the link between the local community and the wider one of Islam.

Fqihs, also called "students" or "seekers after knowledge" (tulba), also serve as prayer-leaders for rural local communities at Friday prayers, write letters or contracts on demand (although after French reforms only authorized notaries could prepare legally binding contracts), provide Quranic recitations at weddings, funerals, and other life crises, and prepare protective amulets. Some fqihs additionally engage in magic (*siḥr*) to influence the course of amorous affairs or the outcome of disputes (e.g., Berque 1955: 316-318, 329, 355), although such practices are considered beyond the pale of Islam (*ḥaram*) by conscientious Muslims.

As professional outsiders with an intimate knowledge of the regions in which they taught and freedom to circulate in rural areas, fqihs constituted informal networks among themselves by which news of openings for Quranic teachers and other information was passed among colleagues. Significantly, in the years immediately prior to Moroccan independence, these networks were used to advantage by the nationalist movement, especially in southern Morocco. Within a decade after independence, the selling of textiles and certain other goods in rural markets and communities in some areas fell almost exclusively into the hands of former Quranic teachers, who took over this activity from departing Jewish traders. The Quranic teachers, like their predecessors, were already clustered into informal networks of trust and cooperation, and had a wide knowledge of the regions in which they worked. Aside from their Jewish predecessors, Quranic teachers constituted the only category of "outsider" ordinarily present in rural society. As "outsiders," they had no direct stake in the local politics of land and water rights (Eickelman 1983).

PLACES OF STUDY

In the larger towns throughout Morocco, students wishing to pursue their studies began by sitting with the circles of men of learning and their disciples that met regularly in the principal mosques (see Laroui 1977b: 196-197, 199-201; Brown 1976: 77). In rural areas, most advanced students continued for at least a few years at one of the numerous madrasas located throughout the country until the early decades of this century (Mouliéras 1895; 1899; Michaux-Bellaire 1911: 436; Waterbury 1972: 30); only a few survive today. Often the level of learning at rural madrasas and zawyas compared favorably with the education obtainable in major urban centers (Berque 1958: 12; Eickelman 1976: 39, 60, 222, 249; as-Susi 1961; Doutté 1914: 269; Mouliéras 1895: 76, 124, 187; 1899: 49, 583).

Such madrasas—and rural zawiyas in many regions—were an essential intermediate stage when Arabic was a student's second language. For many students content with the life of rural Quranic teachers, they could be a final educational stage. In some regions, such as Bzu, these madrasas were only clusters of tents; others were village mosques with adjoining lodgings for the shaykh and his students, who were supported, albeit frugally, by gifts of food from villagers and tribesmen.[6]

---

[6] Until the late nineteenth century, students in rural regions also made collective visits to surrounding villages each year after harvest to collect donations of grain and animals. With these donations, students then camped together and feasted for a week or longer. This practice ceased with the

Most students attended madrasas, often several in succession, as did 'Abd ar-Rahman. The three to five years characteristically spent in this all-male milieu, at least partially removed from their families and communities of origin, was an intense socializing experience. Students often developed close ties with their shaykhs, who could introduce them to scholars elsewhere in Morocco, and with fellow students. This was the case both in 'Abd ar-Rahman's stay in Ait 'Tab, mentioned in the last chapter, and his subsequent one in Dawwar Mshabbak.

In 1927 'Abd ar-Rahman was fifteen years old. His older brother, by then his de facto guardian and Qadi of Bzu, sent him to continue his studies at nearby Dawwar Mshabbak, as he had done earlier. The student body there was a fluctuating one, and students were not constrained to remain for any specific time. Many students simply drifted from encampment to encampment, much as was the pattern in medieval Europe, living a picaresque existence and remaining wherever there was sufficient largesse to maintain them (Aubin 1906: 78-79; Michaux-Bellaire 1911: 437; cf. Ariès 1962: 190-191). To join an encampment, a student approached a mosque at which a fqih was conducting lessons and asked for permission to join them. Hospitality would almost always be offered overnight or for a few days. Longer stays depended upon the resources of the supporting community. Committed students such as 'Abd ar-Rahman sought out specific teachers by their reputation and remained with one teacher long enough to commit to memory and begin to understand some of the principal commentaries and key texts.

'Abd ar-Rahman began to speak Arabic at Dawwar Mshabbak. Its madrasa consisted of several tents, one of which served as a mosque. The students lived five to eight in a tent, with their total number fluctuating between fifteen and thirty. The

---

disorders which accompanied increasing European penetration (Aubin 1906: 78-79; Michaux-Bellaire 1911: 437). The urban counterparts of these outings were the "Feasts of Students."

age of students varied from six to forty, with about half coming from the immediate region and the remainder from Morocco's impoverished south. Some of the more advanced students were simply there waiting for an opportunity to become contracted (*mshārṭ*) as teachers for rural local communities in the region. Others were preparing for higher studies at the Yusufiya.

As at the Ait 'Tab madrasa, student life at Dawwar Mshabbak was intensely communal. Lifelong friendships were forged there. The shaykh and students worked before dawn to perform their ablutions and prepare for the dawn prayer. They then ate together a thick lentil soup (*ḥarīra*). From early morning until just before midday, students individually recited the texts on which they were working. Older students sat with the fqih, who recited and commented upon basic texts. Intermittently the fqih and some of the more advanced students left off their lesson circle to supervise the Quranic memorization of younger students. Lessons stopped just before the midday (*ḍuhr*) prayer, after which students were free to do whatever they wanted until the sunset (*maghrib*) prayers. The evening meal, eaten about an hour and a half after sundown, was donated to the scholars on a rotational basis by households of the rural local community. Afterward, the older and more serious students studied by oil lamps or spoke quietly among themselves. Younger students were expected to do the washing and other chores for older ones in exchange for lessons.

'Abd ar-Rahman's participation in the scholarly community at Dawwar Mshabbak was cut short by a severe drought that affected the region in 1928. He says that conditions were so serious in Bzu's hinterland that tribesmen were reduced to eating a poisonous plant in the region known in tashalhit as *izatti*.[7] In an earlier epoch, the madrasa might have been reconstituted once economic conditions improved, but with the

---

[7] I have been unable to provide further identification for this plant, which 'Abd ar-Rahman knows only by its name in tashalhit.

changed circumstances of the colonial era and the demands for taxes from the colonial administration, the madrasa at Dawwar Mshabbak was unable to recover. 'Abd ar-Rahman continued his studies in Bzu until 16 Rabī'a II 1347/2 October 1928. On that day, carefully recorded in his notebook, he set out for the first time to Marrakesh and studies at the Yusufiya.

FOUR

The Yusufiya: A Profile of Higher Islamic Learning

FOR A Berber youth of sixteen setting out from Bzu in 1928, even if he was the younger brother of the town's qadi, the social universe remained very small. The improved roads and transport of the colonial era had done little to widen it. No Moroccan in Bzu yet owned an automobile, so most local travel was still by mule and horse; 'Abd ar-Rahman set off for the Yusufiya on a mule. His baggage followed on another mule, with a household servant on foot. Once 'Abd ar-Rahman reached the main road at Wād al-'Abīd, he waited for a bus to take him to Marrakesh. 'Abd ar-Rahman had never before been to Marrakesh. Previously he had traveled in the company of his elder brother only to the nearby settlements of Damnat, Azilal, and Sraghna. It would be another decade before he was to travel as far as Casablanca, Rabat, Fez, and Meknes.

Marrakesh in 1928 was composed of the sharply contrasting madina and European *ville nouvelle*, a contrast which is today blurred despite the wall surrounding the old quarters, because the two "separate" towns have grown into one another. As early as 1914, French colonial authorities began to draw up plans to direct the future growth of major Moroccan towns (Abu-Lughod 1980: 146). In Marrakesh as elsewhere, these plans called for the separation of the European "new town" from the "native" quarters. Except for the eventual provision of some piped water, sewers, and electricity, the madina was left "undisturbed." The "new town" of Marrakesh, called Guéliz after a mountain located to its immediate north, was designed with wide avenues radiating from a central point. The main public and commercial buildings were located close to this center, with residential villas located along branching side streets. Guéliz grew modestly through the 1930s and at a more rapid pace only after the Second World War.

In 1928, Marrakesh was still largely encircled almost entirely by palm groves. Today many of these have been cut down to make way for large tracts of popular housing. The wall surrounding its vast madina was built with the reddish clay of the region, which is why the city is affectionately referred to as the "Red City" (*madīnat al-ḥamrā'*). Then as now, Marrakesh is a staging point (and sometimes an end point) for the emigration of Berber-speaking tribesmen from the High Atlas mountains and the Sus river valley. Much of its population is bilingual in Arabic and Berber.

Guéliz was still roughly three kilometers from the walled city of Marrakesh in the late 1920s. At this time, Marrakesh was the largest city in Morocco. It was over one and one-half times the size of Fez and slightly larger than Casablanca. (Like Fez, Marrakesh was to be outstripped in size by the late 1930s by other cities more oriented to industrial and agricultural growth.) Although it was Morocco's largest city, it attracted the fewest Europeans. Except for guided forays of tourists and a few small European enterprises such as carpentry shops, virtually no Europeans entered the madina, and those that did confined themselves to the wider passages. Most went no further than Jamā'a al-Fnā', the main square enlivened by musicians, jugglers, storytellers, beggars, and aspiring guides. Marrakesh lacked major industrial establishments, and European-style education for Muslims was available only on a reduced scale. A French-run School for the Sons of Notables opened in 1919. In contrast to Fez, where a fairly elaborate educational system was in place for the native elite by the 1920s, a secondary school (*collège musulman*) was opened in Marrakesh only in 1936 (French Protectorate 1931: 58, Deverdun 1959: ix).

In the 1920s, Morocco's south still contained pockets of

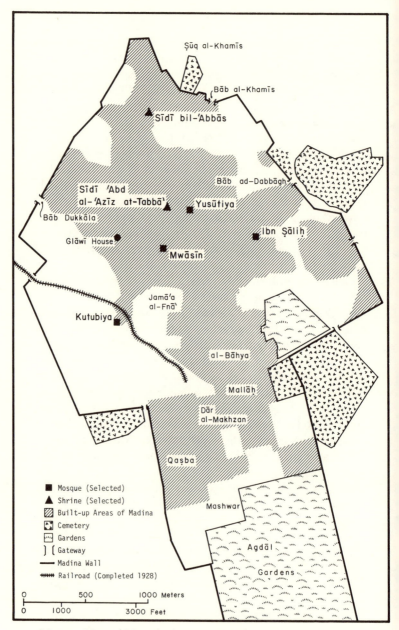

MAP 2. Map of Marrakesh, 1930. Based upon Prosper Ricard,
Le Maroc (Les Guides Bleus), 4th ed. Paris: Librairie
Hachette (1930), p.136.

TABLE 2. THE POPULATION OF MARRAKESH,
CASABLANCA, AND FEZ, 1931

	MARRAKESH		CASABLANCA		FEZ	
	Number	%	Number	%	Number	%
Muslims	167,136	86	85,167	52	95,436	85
Jews	21,607	11	19,960	12	7,826	7
Europeans	6,379	3	57,981	36	9,201	8
TOTAL	195,122	100	163,108	100	112,463	100

SOURCE: 1931 census with corrections (Ricard 1936: 122; Adam 1968: 147). Census figures for the Muslim population were based upon administrative estimates.

resistance to the French. Parts of the High Atlas mountains remained outside effective colonial control until 1933. Their final pacification, together with the earlier quelling of 'Abd al-Krīm's Riffian rebellion in 1927, signalled to all Moroccans the futility of further direct confrontation with colonial authorities. Until 'Abd al-Krim's defeat, many elite of Fez kept their children away from French schools. After his defeat and exile, enrollments soared.

Marrakesh was for centuries the center of the political and economic universe for southern Morocco. With colonial improvements in communications and the decision early in the protectorate to rule the southern region indirectly through tribal strongmen, its political leaders soon became frozen in place for the duration of French rule. The most powerful of the strongmen was Hājj Thāmī al-Glāwī (1879-1956), who emerged as France's principal ally in the south after the death of his elder brother Madanī in 1918. By the late 1920s he was well on his way to consolidating his political control over the entire region, influencing even minor administrative appointments. Although there were few French in Marrakesh, their influence was decidedly felt. It guaranteed the authority of Hajj Thami and his collaborators, over whom the French exercised minimal restraint.

Because of its traditionally high influx of rural immigrants,

Marrakesh has sometimes been described as a city over-
whelmed by its hinterland. This characterization is misleading.
Several of the interior quarters of the madina are as distinguished and exclusive as their equivalents in other "Makhzan"
cities such as Fez and Rabat. As in these cities, at least some
of the elite have chosen to continue living in the madina. Not
far from the Yusufiya mosque-university, for example, is Darb
'Alīlsh, a long, covered impasse in the interior of the madina.
The street is also a cohesive neighborhood. There are no shops
on the street to attract strangers. The nearest ones are on the
"main" street, also inaccessible to vehicles, perpendicular to
Darb 'Alilsh. As with most such quarters, the doors to individual houses give little clue as to the wealth of the inhabitants.
The houses of scholars, wealthy merchants, and craftsmen are
juxtaposed. Persons who enter the street and are unknown to
residents are looked upon with suspicion, for the street is
regarded as a spatial extension of its component households.
Although not all residents of Darb 'Alīlsh have been there for
generations, its population is stable and is composed primarily
of persons born in Marrakesh itself.

Darb Mwāsīn is another such neighborhood, although it is
composed of less prosperous households and is adjacent to
the street of the dyers (Darb Sabbāghīn). Many of its shopkeepers were born in the neighborhood and continue to live
there. Through the 1930s, several distinguished but impecunious men of learning lived there who taught at the Yusufiya.
Darb Mwasin is known architecturally for the mosque that
carries its name, constructed between 1562 and 1573 by a
Sa'ādī dynasty sultan, Sidi 'Abd Allāh bin Muḥammad (r.
1557-1574), and an adjacent fountain which has ceased func-
tioning in recent years from lack of repair. It also contains
the hostel (madrasa: the same term designates any place
where lesson circles are held) for religious students in which
'Abd ar-Rahman spent his seven years in Marrakesh. In contrast to the mosque, the madrasa has been dismissed by an
architectural historian as "without character" and is difficult
even to date (Deverdun 1959: 73). Closed in the early 1950s,

it enjoys today a second life as a government orphanage for girls who claim descent from the Prophet Muhammad.

Older residents and shopkeepers of Darb Mwasin recall that the hostel was an integral part of the neighborhood, even if its students were always thought of as "outsiders" (*āfāqī*; pl. *āfāqīn*). They were often called upon to recite the Quran at appropriate household occasions, and some people regularly brought food to needy students. Religious students of rural origin sometimes developed intimate community ties in Marrakesh. Virtually all the activities associated with the mosque-university were intricately meshed with the wider social and cultural life of the community, a linkage that constituted both a major strength and an inherent limitation upon mosque-university education.

Rural Students in Marrakesh

Rural students were readily distinguished from townsmen by their clothing and what townsmen judged as their awkward comportment. In the 1920s, most students of rural origin, including 'Abd ar-Rahman, still shaved their heads and, as a sign of humility toward their shaykhs, did not wear turbans. This practice had virtually disappeared among younger townsmen, who in general adopted the fez as a sign of modernity. Despite their status as carriers of the Quran, most students were awkward and naive in the ways of the city because of their country origin. Townsmen were not averse to making jokes at their expense when they ventured beyond the immediate confines of the mosque-university and the hostels in which all but the most wealthy "outsider" students, usually of urban origin, were lodged. Nonetheless, some rural students, especially those who came from families of learning, attained scholarly distinction by the most exigent urban standards.

Significantly, two of the most influential reformist shaykhs of the early twentieth century in Morocco, Bū Shu'ayb ad-Dukkālī (1878-1937) and Mukhtar as-Susi (1900-1963), were of rural origin, as were several of the other leading shaykhs of the Yusufiya. Ad-Dukkali was from a rural family that included several generations of men of learning. He first gained attention in Marrakesh at the age of thirteen by reciting all of Sidi Khalil's *Mukhtasar* before Sultan Mulay Hasan I and showing a precocious command of classical Arabic. Later he gained further recognition through studies in Mecca and Cairo. In 1910, at the age of thirty-two, he was appointed qadi of Marrakesh and subsequently became minister of justice (Jirari 1976: 9-18). As-Susi was from a family of learning from the Sus region of Morocco's south, where his father was a leader in the Darqawi religious order. He studied at a rural madrasa in the Sus and from 1919 to 1923 at the Yusufiya, where he was a student of ad-Dukkali and a contemporary of Bzu's Qadi Ahmad. From 1923 to 1927 he was at the Qarawiyin, where he came into contact with most of the later leaders of the nationalist movement. In 1929 he returned to Marrakesh, where his lesson circles were highly popular among students. The French grew suspicious of his growing influence and in 1935 assigned him to forced residence in his natal village in the Sus (Touimi, Khatibi, and Kably 1974: 40-41).

'Abd ar-Rahman and other students from families of rural notables had economic and social advantages in securing ties with persons in the mosque-university milieu that were not available to poorer students. When 'Abd ar-Rahman set out for Marrakesh, his elder brother gave him 600 ryals, an amount that 'Abd ar-Rahman describes as "a lot of money" for the time. His brother also regularly sent him olive oil for cooking, flour, and additional funds as needed. Occasionally his father also sent him money, but not as much.

'Abd ar-Rahman's older brother maintained active ties with several of his former teachers. Upon his arrival in Marrakesh, one of the first things that 'Abd ar-Rahman did was to convey his brother's greetings to his former teachers. One was the reformist shaykh, Bu Shu'ayb ad-Dukkali. Another, more traditionalist, was Muhammad ibn 'Umār as-Sarghīnī (d. 1938), who lectured daily from early morning until late afternoon. By the late 1920s, Muhammad ibn 'Umar was recognized as the leading shaykh of the Yusufiya. When he died, he was buried in the shrine of 'Abd al-'Azīz at-Tabbā', one of the patron marabouts of Marrakesh. 'Abd ar-Rahman recalls that these shaykhs received him cordially, but because of his youth and inexperience, none paid any particular attention to him. In their guest rooms, however, he met other students and scholars whom he presumed by their presence to be serious and of good reputation. In this way he began to discern who was significant in the milieu of higher learning.

STUDENT HOSTELS

Dormitories constituted a significant aspect of the experience of rural students, and for this reason are worth describing in detail. Madrasa students shared many common characteristics and activities. They were unmarried and usually relatively young, between the ages of sixteen and forty. Each hostel usually attracted students from particular regions, as was also the case in Fez (Marty 1924: 337-339).

By the late 1920s, most hostels were suffering from decades of neglect. In principle they were owned and maintained by revenues from pious endowments. Students paid no rents, although they often had to pay key money for rooms, the rights to which could be purchased. Rural students and others from outside Marrakesh also received a daily loaf of bread, the distribution of which was organized by the overseer of a separate pious endowment established for that specific purpose. The occupancy of rooms and the right to a bread allowance were obtained through the spokesman (*mqaddam dyāl at-tulbā*) of each hostel, a student informally selected by his peers for his ability to speak on their behalf when necessary and to see to the fair allocation of bread.

Because of the system of key rights, 'Abd ar-Rahman had no difficulty in securing lodgings upon his arrival. His elder brother had purchased a key to a room at the Mwasin madrasa

TABLE 3. PRINCIPAL MADRASAS AND OTHER LODGINGS FOR
RURAL STUDENTS IN MARRAKESH, 1928–1934

	Founded[a]	Rooms[b]	Students	Region of Origin
Yusufiya (madrasa)	1564/1565	60–70	150–200	Sraghna, Rahamna, Shawiya, Dukkala, Shiyadma
Mwasin (madrasa)	1500–1700	34–38	50	Dukkala, Sraghna, Shiyadma, 'Abda, Sus, Sahara
Ibn Salih	c.1670	6	10	Varied
Bab Dukkala (vacant shops)	c.1700?	25–30	6–8	Unknown
Sidi bil 'Abbas Sabti (shrine with sleeping rooms used by students)	?	?	30–40	Varied
TOTAL		127–146	246–308	

SOURCES: [a] Deverdun 1959: 59, 373, 415, 467; [b] interviews with former students.

from one of his shaykhs a decade earlier.[1] After Ahmad left
the Yusufiya in 1917, he allowed a succession of needy students from the Bzu region to use it until his younger brother
required the room for himself. Such patronage was another
of the multiple ways in which ties were made between persons
in the community of learning. It is also responsible in part for
the tendency of students from the same region to be clustered
together.

The Mwasin was considerably smaller than the nearby Yusufiya madrasa. Its thirty-eight rooms were equally divided
between two stories. In the center of the ground floor was a
fountain for ablutions. In contrast, the Yusufiya hostel is a
vast, imposing structure, with a unified rectilineal design, a
well-lit principal courtyard with a large, oblong basin fed by
underground pipes (qadūs) for ablutions, Andalusian wood-
work, and stucco ornamentation.[2] The rooms were small in

[1] The shaykh was Bu Shu'ayb ash-Shāwī al-Bahlūlī, who was poor and in
need of money. Ahmad's purchase of key rights from him was an indirect
way of contributing to his support.
[2] See Deverdun (1966:II, Pl. 36) for a floor plan.

both madrasas, no more than 1.5 by 2 meters each, and furnished with little more than wooden coffers for the meager possessions of students and sleeping mats, which were placed on the floors or on elevated wooden platforms (*kaṭrīs*). The wooden door of each room had a small opening through which the student's bread ration could be tossed if the student was not present. For lighting, students had small oil lamps that could be placed in a niche in one of the walls. Each room also had a wooden beam in a corner on which clothes could be hung to protect them from mice.

Poor students slept two to three to a room. Wealthier ones such as 'Abd ar-Rahman had rooms to themselves. After residing in the madrasa for several months, 'Abd ar-Rahman acquired two additional rooms, using one for cooking and the storage of foodstuffs, another for sleeping, and retaining his original room for studying.

The life of wealthier students such as 'Abd ar-Rahman was reasonably comfortable. He had regular remittances in cash and kind from Bzu, and cooperated with several other students in paying a man to came to the madrasa daily to do their cooking and washing.

'Abd ar-Rahman and other well-off students regularly shared their food and other resources with poor (*ḍa'īf*) colleagues, who were by far the majority. These students sought in multiple ways to supplement their meager bread ration. Some received a small stipend from pious endowment revenues for reciting the Quran regularly in neighborhood mosques. Others sought out occasions to recite it at weddings, circumcisions, and funerals, for which they received a meal and a modest fee. A few developed client relations with wealthy urban households that provided them regularly with food. Until the early twentieth century in Marrakesh, each religious student also received an annual gift of a jallaba from the sultan on the occasion of the Great Feast ('*Id al-Kabīr*), but this practice ceased with the advent of French rule.

There was sustained community support for higher Islamic learning. Humble artisans and even rural tribesmen periodically came to the Yusufiya to offer gifts of produce, clothes, and other goods to prominent scholars and donations on a smaller scale to needy students. Such actions brought good fortune (*baraka*) to the donor, for whom such donations were considered a pious act (*ihsān*). Wealthy men of learning also contributed. In a 1936 letter, the religious students of Bzu origin in Marrakesh collectively wrote Qadi Ahmad, asking him to contribute money for the Feast of Students. Such requests were regularly made. By the 1940s, "Abd ar-Rahman began to receive similar requests (e.g., letter of 4 Jamada I 1365 / 6 April 1946).

More formal although by no means regular support was provided through pious endowment revenues. A pious endowment was established when a person irrevocably designated the income from a specified property for a pious purpose such as the construction of a mosque or madrasa, its maintenance, the provision of bread for students, a water fountain, the payment of stipends to religious students to recite the Quran regularly, or some equivalent purpose (see Le Tourneau 1949: 465; C. Geertz 1979: 151-154). No new major pious foundations appear to have been established since at least the mid-nineteenth century.[3] Moreover, the economic disruption that accompanied growing European intervention in Morocco had a negative effect upon pious foundation revenues. Nonetheless, successive rulers, local officials, and prominent townsmen saw sporadically to the maintenance and essential repair of mosques, madrasas, and the shrines of key marabouts. Donations for these repairs, like the construction of such buildings in more prosperous eras, was a pious act.

The collection and distribution of pious foundation revenues was supervised in theory by the chief qadi of Marrakesh, who also acted as overseer (nadir) of pious endowment rev-

---

[3] Muhammad Aafif (personal communication) cautions that this prevailing notion of the decline of pious endowments in the nineteenth century may soon change as the result of studies now underway at the Université Muhammad V in Rabat. Until now, no systematic investigation has been undertaken of nineteenth-century source materials.

enues. Given the lack of control over this system, it was inevitable that revenues should be irregularly allocated and often be insufficient to cover the purposes for which they were designated. Often there was no formal accounting at all of income and expenses. Consequently, some madrasas and other buildings simply collapsed from neglect. Deverdun (1959: 567) mentions a madrasa in decrepit condition in the 1850s. No trace of it remained in 'Abd ar-Rahman's time. In practice, each pious foundation had its own administrator. After the protectorate was established in 1912, the French sought to centralize the administration of these revenues and to maintain an accurate inventory of them. According to 'Abd ar-Rahman, the overseer appointed for Marrakesh in the 1920s, a relative of the pasha, had the obvious handicap of illiteracy. Because of ineffective administration, protectorate reforms were slow to come to the Marrakesh region. In Bzu, which was under the formal jurisdiction of Marrakesh for pious endowments, the revenues of each pious endowment continued to be separately administered through the late 1930s.

A description of the role of hostel mqaddams indicates how pious foundations affected the lives of students in practice and and how students were governed. Spokesmen were selected informally by the students of each hostel for an ability to speak effectively on their behalf. In principle, the pasha of Marrakesh or those in charge of disbursing pious endowment funds could object to nominations, but rarely did. In Fez, there appears to have been a formal confirmation from the Makhzan of such spokesmen because they received a small monthly stipend (Le Tourneau 1949: 464). In Marrakesh confirmation was informal. Spokesmen were simply "known" (*ma'rūf*). Thus Ahmad, 'Abd ar-Rahman's elder brother, was spokesman for the Mwasin madrasa during his stay in Marrakesh. He received neither a stipend, which in any case he did not require, nor a formal confirmation of his appointment.

To obtain the bread allowance, each new student paid a small fee to the spokesman, sixty francs as of 1928. The spokesman handed the funds over to the notary responsible for overseeing the distribution of bread to students. The spokesman could also recommend particular students when townsmen came to ask for tulba to recite the Quran for weddings, funerals, and other occasions. It was he who saw to the distribution within the hostel of gifts periodically offered by some wealthy merchants, and the allocation of rooms.

The informal criteria of eligibility to reside in a hostel suggests the unimportance of clearly defined formal authority in the mosque-university milieu. Deverdun (1959: 377) cites the opinion of a fourteenth-century Fassi jurist to the effect that students were obliged to attend lesson circles regularly and were subject to expulsion "by authority" in the case of misconduct or lack of "sufficient aptitude" for studies. One of the few critical cases of expulsion which occurred during 'Abd ar-Rahman's student days indicates how eligibility was withheld in Marrakesh. A Susi student in his late forties had lived for at least two decades at the Mwasin hostel. He was present when Ahmad Mansuri arrived in 1913, and was still there when 'Abd ar-Rahman took up residence in 1928. 'Abd ar-Rahman related:

> In order to get money, he dabbled in magic. So did other students, especially those from the Sus. This meant that quite often he wrote charms for women. He also regularly brought girls and young boys to his rooms. Finally, the students formed a delegation to go to the pasha, Hajj Thami al-Glawi, to have him expelled. We were unsuccessful.

Eventually the collective pressure of the students led to his removal, but the incident underlines the lack of formal authority in student life. The moral authority of shared communal norms was not necessarily backed by formal sanctions. In the past, when the Makhzan provided more regular subsidies to teachers and students alike in the form of stipends—salted beef, grain, oil, and candles (Deverdun 1969: 467; Péretié 1912: 324-334), and rulers such as Mulay Hasan I took a direct interest in the scholarly community, collective activity

84

appears to have been more effective. Nonetheless, the designation of student, literally a "seeker of knowledge" (*tālib 'ilm*), was applied to anyone who had memorized the Quran (or claimed to have done so) and who was oriented toward lifelong religious learning. Such a notion of scholar was highly diffuse, and was shared equally by the scholars of the mosque-university milieu and the wider community.

HIGHER LEARNING AND SOCIETY

A sense of the scale of religious education in the 1920s, however tentative, facilitates understanding how the cultural notion of knowledge was articulated in practice. Traditional higher education was considerably more restricted in scale than Quranic education. In 1931, the year of the first reliable census in the French zone of Morocco, there were approximately 1,200 students in Morocco's two mosque-universities. The country's total population (including estimates for the Spanish zone of influence) was 5,800,000 (Noin 1970: 1, 30, 32), so that mosque-university students constituted a miniscule 0.02 percent of the population.[4] Since most students left their studies after a few years to become merchants, village teachers, notaries, and the like, only a limited number could eventually claim to be men of learning.

The Yusufiya was smaller in scale than its Fez counterpart, and for most of its existence tended to attract students and scholars only from the hinterland of Marrakesh and Morocco's south. Marrakesh first emerged as a major center of learning in the twelfth century, when it rivaled Seville and Cordoba in Muslim Spain. In following centuries its reputation as a center of learning rose and fell with the political vicissitudes of the city itself. Thus it thrived early in the nineteenth century, and again reached national prominence with the residence of

---

[4] In comparison, French secondary education for Moroccan Muslims accounted for 505 students in 1924-1925 and 1,618 students in 1930-1931 (French Protectorate 1931: 245).

the sultan there almost continuously from 1895 to 1901 (Burke 1976: 42, 59). In the late 1920s and early 1930s, the period of immediate concern to this study, the Yusufiya milieu contained roughly four hundred students. Six to eight shaykhs met daily with students in roughly ten lesson circles (*ḥalqa*s).[5]

The Yusufiya, like the Qarawiyin, constituted an institution in the basic sense of a field of activity whose members shared subjectively held ideas and conventions as to how given tasks should be accomplished. Although students and, to a more limited extent, their teachers were only transient members of the community of learning, most persons participated in the mosque-university milieu long enough to give it stability in terms of its participants and their relations with wider society.

The mosque-university's use of space indicates its lack of sharp separation from the rest of society. The activities of the Yusufiya, like those of its counterpart in Fez, were concentrated in space that was shared with the wider community for purposes of worship and other gatherings. Lesson circles of teachers, students, and onlookers met regularly in the Yusufiya (Ibn Yusif) mosque, one of the largest and most central in Marrakesh, as well as in some of the smaller mosques, religious lodges, and at least one shrine, that of the principal marabout of Marrakesh, 'Abd al-'Aziz at-Tabba'. Only the hostels for rural students were reserved exclusively for students.

The Yusufiya had no sharply defined body of students or faculty, administration, entrance or course examinations, curriculum, or unified sources of funds. In fact, its former teachers related with amusement the frustrated efforts of French colonial officials to determine who its "responsible" leaders were and to treat it as a corporate entity analogous to a medieval European university.[6] Although teachers did not act as a for-

---

[5] The Qarawiyin had 700 students in the early 1920s with roughly 40 lesson circles meeting regularly, given by 25 shaykhs (Marty 1924: 345).

[6] Interviews with at-Tuwārtī 'Alī bin Mu'allim, July 25 and 26, 1976.

mal collectivity, several older and respected shaykhs served as informal spokesmen for their colleagues on various occasions. Because of their recognition by the wider community, such individuals in fact controlled the distribution of gifts given by wealthy or powerful individuals to the community of learning. The ability of certain men of learning to control such distributions and to exercise influence on other occasions did much to consolidate their reputations.

The activities of higher learning were integrally related to and limited by the values and expectations of wider society in numerous ways. Teachers were not formally appointed, although some held royal decrees (ḍāhirs) providing them with recognition and specified emoluments. Younger shaykhs simply began to teach after they were assured of the implicit consent of established men of learning capable of sponsoring them and defending them when necessary from the criticism of students and outsiders. The lack of formal appointment meant that shaykhs of lesser reputation had to be especially scrupulous about comporting themselves and commenting on texts in expected ways. Recognition brought most, but not all, teachers small stipends from pious endowments designated for their support, in addition to occasional gifts of grain, olive oil, and clothing from pious townsmen, tribesmen, the sultan, and his entourage.

The publicly accessible activities of the mosque-university did not provide the full range of knowledge, including poetry, history, and literature, or training in the rhetorical style considered essential for men of learning. The formal speech of men of learning was replete with allusions to classical texts and used stylistic conventions that were far removed from ordinary speech. These conventions included the deliberate rhyming of words and phrases and the use of a classicized diction that avoided the intrusion of colloquial or "common" ('ammi) syntax or phrases. Another quality prized by men of learning was the ability to compose verses for particular occasions. These circulated constantly in oral and written form.

Most such poetry drew upon stock formulas, but these still had to be learned and were expected of educated men.[7]

As in any educational system with diffuse, implicit criteria for success and in which essential skills were not fully embodied in formal learning, the existing elite was favored. Moreover, the attribute of "student" did not in itself form much of a basis for meaningful collective action, at least by the late 1920s. Students became "known" as such through their comportment and acceptance by persons in the community of learning, not through any formal procedures. Each student was on his own to discern those persons and ideas that were significant in the world of learning and to create a constellation of effective personal ties with which to function. Students from Marrakesh itself, especially those from wealthy or powerful families, had substantial initial advantages in securing useful ties. They continued to be enmeshed in their families' networks of kinship, friendship, and patronage. Since all students from Marrakesh continued to live at home, those from wealthier and more prestigious families were in a position to invite shaykhs to their homes and to arrange for formal or informal tutoring. Such students often attended the public lesson circles of the mosques and shrines only irregularly.

A significant exception to the diffuse nature of student identity in both Fez and Marrakesh, was the annual "Carnival" or "Feast of Students," introduced in Chapter One. It was an annual occasion on which the sultan and his entourage publicly acknowledged students as a collectivity. Each spring, students solicited contributions from townsmen, and a student was proclaimed "sultan" for the duration of a three-week outing (*nuzha*). The real sultan's parasol, a symbol of authority, was often loaned to the student sultan for the dura-

---

[7] As-Susi's voluminous writings provide particularly useful anthologies of these conventions. Since he was aware that he was documenting a world of learning that was not being transmitted to a younger generation, most of the literary allusions in the writings which he cites are fully annotated, a practice not characteristic of most writings of the period.

tion. The student sultan appointed his peers to offices in his
entourage, mirroring the real Makhzan. The first week of
festivities included a major Friday procession. The next day,
the real sultan's ministers visited their student counterparts
with gifts. Sunday was the turn of the real sultan, before whom
a burlesque Friday sermon (khutba) was delivered. Doutté
(1905: 200) demurely refrains from citing obscene versions
in circulation, but provides others. I translate a brief extract,
lacking the rhyme of the original, from one of his examples:

Praise be to God, Creator of incisors and molars
And who has prepared them to bite into apples and pears
And who has created the hand and the mouth
And who has prepared them to make mouthfuls disappear.
O my brothers, he who eats butter and honey acts well and
proceeds in the good way
And follows the straight path and the just one.
He who eats beans and mallow strays and does wrong
And he harms only his stomach and wrongs no one else.
Worshippers of God,
For he who makes me eat white bread and chicken,
God will open wide the door of Paradise
And he who gives me barley bread and camel meat
Shall share in hell, the worst of soujourns
                    —Doutté 1905: 214-215.

At the end of the sermon, the real sultan gives his student
counterpart cash and gifts so that the students can prolong
their festivities. Doutté also describes in detail the public
processions and provides an inventory of the gifts presented
by the real sultan to the students as a collectivity on one
occasion: thirty-eight sheep, twenty jars of butter, and four
sacks of seminola, in addition to gifts from other officials.[8]

On no other public occasion in Morocco was satire directed

---

[8] Rolleaux-Dugage (1915: 67) mentions in passing that the cost of becoming mock sultan in Marrakesh in 1913 was 1,200 francs, and that the real
sultan presented the student one with a cardboard crown and a horse. For
1919, see the general description of Wattier (1919).

against the protocol of the Makhzan and its authority, which may be one reason why the French brought about its demise. One aspect of the occasion particularly concerned the French. At the very end of his tenure, the student sultan had the right to throw himself at the feet of the real sultan and present him with a list of favors to be granted. One reason that wealthy merchants often subsidized the bidding of their candidates for the role was that the favors granted could be quite substantial. According to Cénival (1925: 139), the cost of purchasing the right to becoming student sultan escalated in Fez from 750 francs in 1916 to 4,000 in 1917, 22,500 in 1923, and 13,250 in 1924. The unusually high figure for 1923 was caused by a qaid who wanted the student sultan to ask that a member of his family be appointed as his deputy; the request was refused. In 1925 the protectorate administration forbade seeking favors of the real sultan during the carnival. As a result, the auction price for the privilege of becoming mock sultan in Fez immediately fell to 1,350 francs. Comparable figures for Marrakesh are unavailable.

Although the French sought to discourage the Feast of Students, it continued to thrive in Marrakesh throughout 'Abd ar-Rahman's stay. For most of his years there, the Sultan of the Students was from Dukkala. Religious students from that region were given bridewealth and a home if they returned as Sultan of the Students, so competition was intense. Some students prolonged their stay in Marrakesh in order to be selected. Although the pasha did not attend the event personally, presumably at the instigation of the French, his deputy was present and provided funds, soldiers, and the loan of a horse.

'Abd ar-Rahman usually returned to Bzu during the time of the Feast of the Students, but he remained in 1928 because a friend of his, Si 'Umar ad-Dukkali, became mock sultan. After his week as sultan in Marrakesh, Si 'Umar returned to Dukkala. 'Abd ar-Rahman accompanied him. Once they arrived at the house of the qaid of the region, they were entertained lavishly and then provided with a car and a tribal guard of honor for the remainder of the journey.

THE MOSQUE-UNIVERSITY MILIEU

Students acquired the necessary knowledge and personal contacts to achieve reputations as men of learning through three overlapping spheres of activity: lesson circles; peer learning, including participation in student literary circles; and sponsorship by established men of learning. The first and third spheres are familiar elements in accounts of Islamic education. Peer learning is not, since traditional Arabic sources have stylistic conventions that render them almost entirely silent on informal patterns of learning. Thus, when several Moroccan men of learning were asked to prepare short written autobiographies (tarjamas), they mentioned only learning derived from their shaykhs, in conformity with explicit cultural assumptions concerning the proper acquisition and transmission of learning.

Lesson Circles

The spatial and temporal setting of formal learning is highly significant in suggesting the relation of religious knowledge to society at large. Almost all of the lesson circles that met in the daytime were held in the Yusufiya mosque itself and concerned the most traditional and accepted texts of jurisprudence, grammar, and rhetoric. They were conducted by shaykhs regarded as the most senior and conventional. Evening lesson circles were usually held only in shrines, religious lodges, and smaller mosques. These were conventionally devoted to less established subjects and texts, and were generally conducted by reformist shaykhs and those of reformist sympathies, although a few were also conducted by shaykhs who lectured in the daytime at the Yusufiya.

Daytime lesson circles met five times weekly, Saturdays through Wednesdays. The shaykhs who conducted these lesson circles usually also conducted lesson circles on Thursday and Friday mornings, but would comment on different texts. During the major religious holidays, commentary on the regular texts were also suspended. The holidays were 'Ashura, the tenth day after the start of the Muslim New Year; the Prophet's birthday ('Īd Milūd); Ramadan, the lunar month of fasting; and the period of the Great Feast, from 25 Dhū Qa'ada in the lunar calendar to 25 Dhū Hijja. The texts commented upon during these periods included panegyrics on the Prophet, biographical literature on him, and commentaries on the sayings and actions of the prophet (hadīth). Rural students took advantage of the longer holidays to return to their regions of origin, so that at these times the audiences of shaykhs was less rurally oriented than they were for the rest of the year.

As in the rest of Marrakesh, mosque-university activities were organized around the daily cycle of prayers. 'Abd ar-Rahman's schedule appears to have been fairly representative of that of serious rural students. He woke up just before dawn to perform his ablutions and prayers. Then he read and memorized in his room until eight in the morning, when the first lesson circles began at the Yusufiya. Each was attended by ten to thirty regular students, depending upon the popularity of the shaykh. The first lesson circles of the day concerned jurisprudence. Throughout his six years at the Yusufiya, 'Abd ar-Rahman followed the lessons of Shaykh Muhammad ibn 'Umar as-Sarghini on Ibn Ishaq's *Mukhtasar*. Indicative of the lack of "closure" in traditional studies, Ibn 'Umar was unable to complete his commentary on the entire treatise in the six years that 'Abd ar-Rahman followed his lessons.

A second group of lesson circles began mid-morning. These were primarily concerned with grammar, and 'Abd ar-Rahman followed the commentaries of Shaykh Ahmad Agurram, a Berber of rural origin, who commented on Ibn Malik's *Alfiya*. The midday prayers marked the beginning of the next cycle of lesson circles, when 'Abd ar-Rahman returned to Shaykh Muhammad ibn 'Umar for his commentary on texts dealing with grammar, rhetoric, and the conjugation of verbs—sciences that were important, 'Abd ar-Rahman explained, in order to establish the precise meaning of utterances. Following the mid-afternoon ('asr) prayers, 'Abd ar-Rahman joined Shaykh Mulay Aḥmad al-ʿAlamī for his commentaries upon Ibn ʿAsim's *Tuḥfa* and, in later years, his Quranic exegesis, a subject that was then being reemphasized in the lesson circles of the Yusufiya under the stimulus of reformist shaykhs.

There was more flexibility in the content and conduct of the lesson circles that met after the sunset prayers. After sunset, Shaykh Muhammad ibn ʿUmar went to a small mosque in a fort (*qaṣr*) situated next to the royal palace, where he lectured on Ibn Abī Zayd's *Risāla*, a twelfth-century legal text characterized by Berque (1949: 75) as a "juridical vegetation of practical applications, cases in point, and legal justifications." The reformist shaykh, Mukhtar as-Susi, regularly lectured evenings at the shrine of ʿAbd al-ʿAzīz at-Tabbaʿ and in the Darqawi religious lodge, which also served as his residence. He even commented upon texts of poetry, including the *Maqāmāt* of al-Ḥarīrī and occasionally lectured in colloquial Arabic, so that his lectures could be widely understood.

The conduct of lesson circles in public settings, where they were accessible to nonstudents at all times, indicated popular support of and respect for the activities of learning, but also imposed implicit constraints upon what was learned and the conduct of the lessons. Leading shaykhs were publicly treated with deference and respect as they walked through the streets; their hands were kissed, and it was not unusual for gifts to be offered them by pious townsmen and villagers. As another indication of respect, many merchants and craftsmen regularly attended lesson circles for the religious merit they felt such participation would bring, despite the fact that few of them could follow the classical Arabic in which they were presented. Nonetheless, their presence restricted the introduction of unfamiliar material in lesson circles, informal discussions between teachers and students, and anything that deviated from popular expectations of what was "proper" for such activities.

Propriety of form obliged shaykhs to adhere to the rhetoric of classical Arabic and to comment only upon the texts of others. The formal necessity to do so, no matter how urgent some considered the political issues of the day to be (Berque

1974: 174-175), constrained both reformist and other shaykhs to stress that they spoke less for themselves than in their roles as transmitters of a fixed body of knowledge. As Bloch (1975: 16) has observed, at a high level of rhetorical formality, the content of speech and the order in which material is arranged are not seen "as the result of the acts of anybody in particular, but of a state which has always existed." Such form is, of course, congruent with the paradigm of mnemonic (and popularly legitimate) learning. The same level of formality is apparent in the preparation of tarjamas. The impersonal nature of the tarjama's literary form, in which the third person is used both for biographies and autobiographies, reinforces the formal ideological conviction that religious knowledge is transmitted intact from generation to generation without alteration by persons or events. But although the words could be the same, meaning could shift, and the use of some texts and the neglect of others could be used to make a statement on contemporary events. Only those with a sophisticated command of such textual nuances could follow the meaning of the lecturer first-hand.

In practice, shaykhs could introduce a wide variety of material into their commentaries, but the base of the educational process was still a set of texts that took years to memorize and even more time to use actively in discourse. In itself, the form of commentaries did not limit innovation in subject matter and adaptation to change, except that it deflected attention from awareness of historical and contextual transformations.

The form of lesson circles conveyed the notion of the fixity of knowledge by minimizing active student contributions and by providing no checks upon what students understood. Only the student chosen as reader (*sārid*) of the text to be commented upon took an active role. As this task was rarely rotated, few students acquired even this experience. The shaykh interrupted the student's reading only to correct errors of vocalization and to deliver his commentary. As with Greek and Latin literature in medieval Europe, the transmission of a text entailed taking it by dictation from someone reputed to know its proper form, so as to prevent the accretion of errors (Reynolds and Wilson 1974). More significantly, however, only the oral transmission of knowledge was regarded as culturally legitimate in the Moroccan context; knowledge acquired exclusively from the study of books, as in classical Greece (Ong 1981) was considered unreliable. Interruption of student readings was a way of signaling important points, and verbal emphases could be used to communicate more than a written text could convey. Significantly, the introduction of printed texts after 1865 (al-Manuni 1974: 207-213) had minimal impact upon the form of the lesson circles. No questions were asked during these sessions, and students rarely took notes or made annotations in the printed copies of texts that a few possessed. Former students explained that deference and propriety toward their shaykhs prevented their openly raising any issues. Questions had to be placed indirectly, usually in private as the shaykh prepared to leave the mosque or shrine, so as not to suggest a public challenge to his scholarship (see also Delphin 1889: 28). Moreover, as former students emphasized, informal contact with their shaykhs to discuss specifically textual matters was exceptional. Thus there were no significant practical opportunities for students to use the concepts or materials they sought to learn under the guidance of their shaykhs.

A parenthetical comment is essential here. There is no reason to assume, as many scholars have, that latter-day Islamic higher education in Morocco was a "decayed" remnant of earlier periods. Intra-Islamic differences noted by Ibn Khaldun have already been mentioned. In Morocco at least, the educational process was never fully encompassed within the public activities of lesson circles. In other countries lesson circles sometimes were arenas for long-term dialogues between teachers and their students (e.g., Snouck Hurgronje 1931: 190; Fischer 1980a: 61-103; Makdisi 1981); this pattern is only one of several that Islamic education has taken, although it has often incorrectly been assumed to be normative for the entire Islamic world. Thus there were several patterns of Islamic education, of which the Moroccan emphasis upon mne-monic possession is but one realized form. Indeed, when some reformers decided in Fez that French should be added to the curriculum of religious students—it was never added at the Yusufiya—study of this foreign language took the character-istic form of memorized verses, in Arabic script:

ṣabaḥ al-khayri ʿindahum "Bonjour"
wa-in ʾardta ṭūl ad-dawāmi qul "Toujours"
as-suʾāl ʿan al-ḥāl ʿindahum "Comment ça va?"
wa-l-jawābu ʿind al-ghāya "Ça va."[9]

"Good morning" among them is *Bonjour*,
To express forever say: *Toujours*,
Asking "How's it going?" among them is *Comment ça va?*
And the reply to that is *Ça va.*

Reformist shaykhs sought to introduce new material into lesson circles and to draw students into a critical questioning of the relation of Islam to contemporary society (Merad 1971). A description and analysis of the context of their lesson circles and the extent to which they were innovative indicate the constraints that the public and religious conception of valued knowledge placed upon the potential for adaptation. Former students of the period, including ʿAbd ar-Rahman, spoke en-thusiastically of the reformist shaykhs as having "liberated" (ḥarrar) them from what they regarded as commentaries upon a narrow range of subjects that had remained unchanged for three or four hundred years. Such hyperbolic claims accurately reflect the attitude of students, but reformist teachings fit well within the "prismatic" nature of Islamic learning. A compar-ison of lists of texts commented upon at different periods from the late nineteenth to the early twentieth century indicated regular variations in both subjects and texts (Delphin 1889: 30-41; Michaux-Bellaire 1911: 434-449; Péretié 1912: 334-345; Marty 1924: 345-347; Berque 1949).

---

[9] I am grateful to Muhammad Aafif for providing this example.

In practice, the principal achievement of the reformers of the 1920s was to introduce material into lesson circles that men of learning earlier had privately acquired in the houses of the elite: Quranic exegesis, theology, history, and classical poetry and literature (*adab*). The reformers argued that these topics were as much a part of the religious sciences as those subjects that had been taught conventionally in Morocco prior to their time (as-Susi 1961: IX, 167-168), a contention that engendered animosity from more traditionalist shaykhs. As Mukhtar as-Susi gained in popularity at the Yusufiya during the late 1920s, men of learning opposed to him went to the pasha and attributed to him the claim that he saw himself as another mahdi like Ibn Tumārt (d. 1130), the Berber religious reformer and founder of the Almohad (*al-Muwāḥidūn*) movement, who modeled his life on that of the Prophet Muhammad and who saw himself as the Prophet's spiritual heir. As-Susi's detractors also claimed, with some contradiction, that he had students read poetry about women and drinking, not about religion. His more modernist detractors told students inclined to support him that they were not modernists (*'asriyūn*) but left-handed (*'isriyūn*), those who were not following the right path of Islam. The allusion to left-turning referred to left-handed locks, those that did not conform to accepted patterns, and not to the political left of European politics. Such borrowed allusions became prevalent only later.

Despite reformist innovations and efforts to instil a new critical approach to the religious sciences that went beyond the assimilation of received texts and tradition, knowledge continued to be legitimized by indicating how it fitted within the established religious sciences. It also had to be conveyed in classical Arabic, which limited its accessibility to the same select few who participated in traditional Islamic education. Reformists made some use of colloquial Arabic, an immensely popular innovation, but mostly on the occasion of religious holidays.

The political authorities were aware how easily lessons in colloquial Arabic could become a formidable political vehicle.

Nonetheless, even reformist shaykhs, to seek legitimacy for their teachings, lectured within the range of popularly expected places and times. The fact that they lectured only after the sunset prayers, a time set aside for the more peripheral religious sciences or for less established shaykhs, and in locales such as religious lodges and smaller mosques, signaled to all but their immediate followers that their teachings were not symbolically as central as the "core" components of the religious sciences taught during the day at the Yusufiya. Within the restricted group of mosque-university students, reformist shaykhs enjoyed a considerable following, despite the active opposition of many of the more traditional shaykhs, who were frequently backed by support of the public and the political authorities. In the context of the lesson circles, the reformists did little to make their teachings accessible to a wider audience or fundamentally to change prevalent understandings of the forms in which valued knowledge was conveyed.

Peer Learning

Peer learning has been neglected in the study of many educational systems, including Western ones, because it is characteristically informal.[10] In Morocco it provided what public lesson circles could not—an active engagement with and practice in the comprehension of basic texts. For most rural students, peer learning had special importance, since such students were usually even more cut off than their urban counterparts from initiating informal contacts with their shaykhs, especially during the earlier years of their studies. Even in urban milieus, reading and writing were often learned from peers and not from formal education.

[10] The overall neglect of the importance of peer learning (e.g., Makdisi 1981) in studies of Islamic education is still remarkable, even considering the silence of traditional sources. McLachlan (1974: 474) describes a similar neglect in the study of colleges in early nineteenth-century America, despite the fact that the core of learning during this period was "an extraordinarily intense system of education by peers."

'Abd ar-Rahman's experience in Marrakesh indicates the significance of peer learning. For the first three months after his arrival in Marrakesh, he lived alone at the Mwasin and gradually got to know which of his fellow students were intent upon their studies. In the room above him, for example, was a Susi, Sī Muḥammad Tanānī, who later got a job working for the Ministry of Justice; he read in his room until as late as one in the morning. "I could tell because there was a light on his room for all that time." During his early months in Marrakesh, 'Abd ar-Rahman continued to visit the shaykhs with whom his brother studied, including Bu Shu'ayb ad-Dukkali. One of the fellow students he met during one visit to Bu Shu'ayb was Sī Muḥammad bin Ṭālib ad-Dukkālī, an older, impecunious student who was also living at the Mwasin. Because Si Muhammad was also from Dukkala and was a co-guest with Shaykh Bu Shu'ayb, 'Abd ar-Rahman assumed that the two scholars from Dukkala were "close" (qrib), another indication of Si Muhammad's integrity. 'Abd ar-Rahman explained how Si Muhammad came to share his rooms:

Si Muhammad (d. 1946) was a great man of learning who never spoke unless it was necessary. The Quran was always on his lips. He lived from the daily bread given rural students and from the daily eight francs he received for reciting [the Quran] at a mosque. I observed his conduct for some time. Finally, I spoke to him and said that I was a beginner [in the religious sciences] and wanted someone to live with me who could help me in my studies. So I gave him the key to one of my rooms and said it was his. I wanted nothing in return except the opportunity to speak with him about the books I was reading. Si Muhammad was in his thirties and I was sixteen or seventeen when we began to live together. Whenever he needed a little money, I gave it to him.

What I had been doing until I met him was memorizing books, but without understanding what I read. We worked alone for the first several months that we lived together. Then, although I was a newcomer to Marrakesh, students who had been there for years asked *me* to read with them. They saw that I was a serious student and wanted to study with me.

For seven years I lived with Si Muhammad. . . . This was the real learning that I did in my years at the Yusufiya. Of course I learned much at the lesson circles, but it was in reading texts (*al-mutūn*) with Si Muhammad and with other students and in explaining them to each other that most of the real learning went on.

After he left the Yusufiya in the mid-1930s, Si Muhammad became a minor official with the Ministry of Justice and married a daughter of the qadi of Dukkala, his region of origin. Some men of learning in Marrakesh are less admiring of Si Muhammad's scholarly credentials; one described him to me as an ordinary, plodding rural fqih. Such an evaluation in no way vitiates the fact that he provided 'Abd ar-Rahman with what the public lesson circles could not: an active engagement with and comprehension of the basic texts.

Knowledge of basic texts, however, was sufficient qualification only for modest positions as notaries or village teachers, though it was the terminal stage of learning for all but a few students. The additional knowledge considered essential for men of learning and the practice necessary to develop competent rhetorical style took place in a complementary form of peer learning—the small, ephemeral literary circles to which a large number of the more successful students belonged.[11] These literary circles flourished especially with the rise of the proto-nationalist movement in the late 1920s, but similar groups existed in earlier periods and were by no means unique to Morocco (Delphin 1889: 27, 53; Heyworth-Dunne 1968: 13, 40, 66). Participants in these circles read and discussed

[11] Unlike 'Abd ar-Rahman, Si Muhammad belonged to none of these associations.

the Moroccan literary magazines (e.g., *Majallat al-Maghrib* and *Majallat as-Salām*) that had begun to emerge during this period, Moroccan newspapers and those of the Arab East (banned by the French), books on subjects such as history (including that of Morocco), geography, poetry, and their own compositions.

As was the case with other aspects of higher Islamic education, student literary circles were weak in organizational form and dissolved frequently. Most were relatively small, with a dozen or so members, and usually met daily, after the sunset prayers. 'Abd ar-Rahman belonged to the "League of Goodness and Fortune" (*jām'iyat al-khayr wa-s-sadād*), which lasted for about six months in 1932, until it was forced to dissolve by agents of the pasha. Although it was referred to in formal Arabic as a "league" or "association" (jami'a), 'Abd ar-Rahman informally referred to the group as a *ṭā'ifa*, using a word associated with religious lodges, which the League resembled in form. The League's informal leader was Ibrāhīm al-Ilghī, a younger brother of the reformist shaykh Mukhtar as-Susi, who rented a small house adjacent to his brother's Darqawi religious lodge for the use of the group. A small fine was levied on members whenever they missed a meeting, the proceeds of which paid for a meal that its members shared each Friday after the communal prayers, a practice also common to the religious brotherhoods of the period.

The League of Goodness and Fortune, like other peer associations, provided a training ground for debating, speaking, and writing within the conventions of formal Arabic. Relations among its members approached equality, so that participants took turns in delivering speeches which were subjected to the criticism of the group.

To indicate the tenor of these speeches, 'Abd ar-Rahman showed me a notebook containing a speech that he presented to the League. The aim of the speech was to defend Marrakesh against the charge that it was not a major cultural center because so many of its inhabitants were Berber-speakers and because it had a smaller community of learned men than Fez.

In alliterative, rhymed prose, 'Abd ar-Rahman defended Marrakesh by describing its physical beauty and its great poets and men of letters, both past and contemporary. The speech further enumerates the major marabouts (ṣāliḥūn) associated with Marrakesh, confirming the lack of a sharp dichotomy in the early 1930s between a reform-minded Islam and a more popular form in which local maraboutic beliefs were considered to be an integral part of Islam (see Eickelman 1976: 211-230). The speech concludes by exuberantly labeling Marrakesh the "Baghdad of the Maghrib." Most of the speech consists of conventional platitudes, but its content, diction, and syntax reflect a style mastered only by the traditionally educated.[12]

Some literary circles, especially those influenced by reformist ideas such as the League of Goodness and Fortune, were concerned to a limited extent with undertaking political action for the benefit of the wider Islamic community. Carriers of religious knowledge regarded themselves as legitimate spokesmen for Islam, and were popularly regarded as such. This was especially the case after the "Berber Proclamation" of 1930, by which the French formally extracted certain Berber-speaking regions of Morocco from the jurisdiction of Islamic law courts. This event had repercussions throughout the Islamic world as a symbol of the efforts of European colonial powers to weaken Islam. The practical influence of men of learning, sharply circumscribed since the advent of colonial rule, temporarily reemerged with this event. In some Moroccan cities, including Fez, protests organized against this proclamation were overtly political and occasionally violent (see Brown

---

[12] A quality praised by men of learning was the ability to compose verses for particular occasions such as appointments to government posts, weddings, and the birth of children. There was a constant circulation of such commemorative verses orally and in writing among men of learning. Most such poetry involved little originality, as its creators drew upon stock phrases, conventions, and images, but these creations deliberately avoided the diction and syntax of "commoner" speech.

1973: 201-215; 1976: 198-206). In general, however, protests took traditional and nonviolent forms such as public communal prayers similar to those in cases of drought or other natural disasters. Many of these prayers were organized by literary circles. In Marrakesh, firmly under the control of its pasha, Hajj Thami al-Glawi, demonstrations were rapidly quelled. Students with ties to urban and rural notables were warned in advance by their relatives to stay removed from the "troubles." Said 'Abd ar-Rahman:

A few days before the Berber proclamation, a messenger came to me from [my elder brother in] Bzu. He said that something big was going to happen in a few days and to stay away from it by remaining in the hostel. I didn't know what it was. I thought that perhaps it had to do with a film the Jews were making.[13]

I remained in my rooms, but many of the other students went into the streets to demonstrate. Soldiers (*makhaznis*) from the pasha arrested many of them and took them to prison. Later, much later, some of the men of learning went to the pasha to plead for the students' release, and most of them were. I wanted to continue my studies and these demonstrations had nothing to do with my studies.

Participants in several literary circles nonetheless took action that could at least formally be construed as nonpolitical. One such action taken by the League of Goodness and Fortune was for its members to persuade individually (to avoid suspicions of organized group activity) the men who gathered each evening in the town's mosques to recite the Quran in

---

[13] Because the Alliance Israélite had been active since the nineteenth century in Marrakesh in providing education in French to Moroccan Jews, many had become clerks and interpreters for the protectorate government and commercial interests. If indeed a film was then being prepared in Marrakesh, it would have been perceived as having been organized by "Jews," because local Jewish interpreter/assistants would have been the most readily available and the only personnel of any film crews likely to be able to converse in Arabic.

unison instead of separately, as had been the practice, in order to symbolize the unity of Islam. In this activity they were successful, but the pasha's police soon discovered who instigated it. Some leading religious scholars vouched for the intentions of the League's members, so they avoided arrest. Still, they were compelled to give up their meeting place and refrain from meeting in the future.

The narrow range of political actions undertaken by participants in lesson circles and even student associations suggests the restricted vision of public responsibility associated with the Islamic tradition of "gentlemanly" education as elaborated in Morocco. A man of learning's primary responsibility was to acquire religious knowledge and to use it in prescribed ways, not to seek to alter the shape of society. Reformist Muslim intellectuals in North Africa, stimulated at least in part by the fact of European political dominance, challenged many aspects of Islam as it was locally understood, both popularly and in educated circles, but they fell short of offering ideological and practical alternatives to the existing social order. Reformist teachings in the 1930s offered no alternative to the accepted popular notion of social inequality as a "natural" fact of the social order, nor did they elaborate a wider notion of social responsibility to men of learning than that of perfecting their own understanding of religious knowledge and communicating it to relatively restricted circles (Merad 1971: 193-227; Eickelman 1976: 126-130).

Sponsorship

Students remained in the milieu of learning for as long as they chose or were able to. Just as there were no formal markers of entry to this milieu, there were none upon leaving it. Only a few students managed to acquire reputations as men of learning. There were no explicit criteria by which recognition could be achieved, so education could not assume the function of "certification" so closely associated with modern Western institutions.

One means, however, of signaling the completion of studies was for a student to ask each of his shaykhs for a "teaching license" (*ijāza*). Such documents specified the texts or subjects studied and the qualifications of the teacher. In Morocco and throughout the Islamic world, teaching licenses were only as good as the reputations of their writers and the facility with which their bearers could use them (cf. Heyworth-Dunne 1968: 67-69; Makdisi 1981). As 'Abd ar-Rahman commented, one sought ijazas from those shaykhs who "had God's blessings in the religious sciences and feared God the most, those who were older and more powerful and who always had their hands kissed in the street." In practice, many outstanding students of the period, especially those from Marrakesh itself, claim that they deliberately did not ask for such documents; many were prepared as mere courtesies for educated rural notables, and not to possess them could in some circumstances be a mark of higher status. What counted was sponsorship and active recognition by established men of learning and the effective use to which an individual could put such ties as well as those with other persons of influence.

Since the world of learning was not a closed community, support in nonlearned environments could also be decisive in acquiring a reputation for learning. As indicated in the following chapter, Moroccan men of learning of the generation of the 1930s have significant ties with each other, created in part through common schooling; but these ties are not exclusive, and overlap with social bonds created on other bases. Social recognition as a man of learning is an attribute that is used variously according to social context. In Morocco such persons constitute a social type rather than a distinct group that has sharply defined boundaries or that acts collectively now or did so in the past (Brown 1976: 75-81; Burke 1976: 218; cf. Eickelman 1976: 89-91, 183-189).[14]

[14] For discussion of Islamic men of learning in other cultural contexts in the Muslim world, see Baer (1971), Bulliet (1972), Green (1976), Hourani (1968), Keddie (1972), Lapidus (1967), Mottahedeh (1975, 1981), and Saad (1983).

The majority of students rarely used religious knowledge in more than an iconic fashion, as a marker of one-time participation in the milieu of learning. When I asked former students about the fact that most left their studies prior to acquiring scholarly recognition, there was often a formal expression of regret but none of failure attached to such attrition. In discussing their years at the mosque-university, most emphasized the opportunities they created to secure ties with persons within and outside the community of learning. These ties often were of use later in facilitating commercial, political, and entrepreneurial activities. The frequency with which such ties were mentioned suggests an implicitly shared conception of career, although not in the narrowly occupational sense of the term. When I asked former students what their goals were at the time of their studies, most replied that they were concerned primarily with the acquisition of the religious sciences. This was to be expected, given the cultural emphasis upon such valued knowledge. Acquiring the religious sciences additionally implied participation in social networks with persons drawn from different backgrounds and regions of Morocco, and thus with actual or potential access to a wide range of centers of power. No other preparation, except perhaps association with the Sultan's entourage, enabled a person to acquire such a wide range of potential associations. Knowledge of the religious sciences was, of course, essential at some level in order to function as a qadi, a notary, a scribe with the government, or a teacher in the religious sciences. Acquiring such knowledge also provided the consociational base from which a wide range of extralocal political, economic, and social activities could be undertaken, at least so long as there were no major alternatives to Islamic higher education.

FIVE

The World of the Educated
Rural Notable

"I received," says Husserl, "the education of a German, not that of a Chinaman. But my education was also that of the inhabitant of a small town, with a home background, attending a school for children of the lower middle class, not that of a country landowner's son educated at military college."
—cited in Bourdieu 1967: 358

In the beginning of 1354 (April 1935), ['Abd ar-Rahman] unwillingly returned to Bzu because his brother Ahmad (may God comfort him) appointed him as notary and deputy (nā'ib) without prior consultation. He intended to continue steadfastly in his studies but his hopes in this were extinguished. Circumstances did not otherwise permit."
—Tarjama, November 20, 1976

THE RETURN

One morning in April 1935, the car and driver of the qaid of Azilal, Qadi Ahmad Mansuri's father-in-law, arrived unexpectedly in Marrakesh. The driver had orders to take 'Abd ar-Rahman immediately to Azilal. Through friends traveling from Bzu to Marrakesh, 'Abd ar-Rahman knew that a notary in Bzu had recently died and that there was no other qualified notary of Bzu origin to take his place. He was also aware that his elder brother intended to appoint him to keep the post from going to an "outsider" (barrānī).

'Abd ar-Rahman arrived at the Native Affairs Administration (*Contrôle*) building in Azilal later that day and was immediately ushered into the office of the French officer; his brother was also there. The officer took one look at 'Abd ar-Rahman and said that he was too young for the post. He was only twenty-two at the time. After further discussion, the captain finally allowed 'Abd ar-Rahman to proceed to Rabat to be examined by the minister of justice on his knowledge of Islamic law and to leave the final decision to Rabat officialdom. A mere notary could be examined and confirmed in Marrakesh, but appointment to the post of deputy qadi, even if unpaid except in the case of the qadi's absence, could be made only in Rabat.

Late that afternoon, 'Abd ar-Rahman left Azilal. He stayed overnight in Casablanca and at dawn proceeded to Rabat. As a religious student with little experience of the world beyond Marrakesh, 'Abd ar-Rahman had no clear notion of the hours of government offices. At seven in the morning, he arrived by mistake at the door of the Direction des Affaires Chérifiennes, the French-directed section of the protectorate administration charged with "advising" the sultan and the "Moroccan" ministries, which included the Ministry of Justice. After an hour's wait, a porter (*shāwsh*) arrived and brusquely directed him, in a manner reserved for persons of country appearance, to the Dār al-Makhzan, where the Ministry of Justice was located.

At the Dar al-Makhzan, 'Abd ar-Rahman showed his letter from the Native Affairs Officer in Azilal to another porter and explained the purpose of his visit. So that he would be properly attired for the interview, Ahmad had lent his younger brother a *silhām*, a light cloak worn over the jallaba on formal occasions. 'Abd ar-Rahman had no idea how to wear it, so simply draped it over his shoulders. The porter grabbed it from him and forced it over his head in the proper manner, then directed him to another porter. After another long wait, 'Abd ar-Rahman was ushered into a room with seven Moroccan "scribes" (*kātibs*), seated on low-lying benches arranged along the walls of the room. In a curious attempt to preserve the "authenticity" of the "Moroccan" ministries, the French discouraged desks and chairs.

In retrospect, 'Abd ar-Rahman admits with amusement that he did not cut an imposing figure. In the rapidly disappearing fashion of a rural religious student, his head was shaved and he wore no turban. His appearance alone was sufficient to amuse sophisticated Makhzan officials. They asked 'Abd ar-Rahman where he was from, and he showed them the papers he had been given in Azilal. Teasing him, the clerks asked him how a Berber like himself learned to speak proper Arabic. 'Abd ar-Rahman answered that he had memorized the Quran, so of course he could speak a correct Arabic. Then they asked him a number of historical questions, including the names of the founders of Morocco's dynasties. The officials clapped their hands each time he answered correctly, saying how pleased they were to find a Berber notary who also knew history. Their other questions were more directly related to notarial tasks, including the fine points of formulaic phrases that notaries used in their work. 'Abd ar-Rahman was not familiar with all of these, but he managed to answer to the satisfaction of his questioners. Finally they teased him about whether he knew how to prepare a marriage contract, saying that he was too young to be expected to possess such knowledge.

After an hour of questioning, 'Abd ar-Rahman was told to leave the room. A porter escorted him outside the building to wait a further summons. After an interval, the porter beckoned to him, saying that the Moroccan minister of justice had arrived, but that the French delegate to the Ministry of Justice was not yet present. After another wait, 'Abd ar-Rahman was called inside and made to sit in a chair between the minister and the French delegate. The minister asked him to read aloud and explain about fifteen lines of a text on jurisprudence. Other questions included explaining the meaning of "to judge" (*qadā*) in Arabic and the six conditions necessary for a qadi properly to perform his tasks.

At first, the "Christian" delegate remained silent.[1] Then he posed, in Arabic, a problem in inheritance (mirāth): "If a man dies and leaves a full sister (by his mother and father) and a sister by his father only, how is the inheritance divided?" 'Abd ar-Rahman gave the proper answer: "The full sister was entitled to half, the half-sister to one sixth of the inheritance." At this point, the "Christian"—'Abd ar-Rahman could not further identify him—indicated his agreement to the appointment and left the room. The minister then told him that he was pleased with his answers, and informed 'Abd ar-Rahman that a proclamation confirming his appointment as deputy to his brother would be issued.

'Abd ar-Rahman left immediately for Casablanca. His older brother was waiting for him there, together with Ḥasan al-Bū Naʿmānī, a poet and a friend of 'Abd ar-Rahman.[2] He wrote a twenty-two-line poem, a qaṣīda, for the occasion, the first line of which reads, "You gave me good news in the morning, then he walked in proudly" (Naba' 'atānī fī aṣ-ṣabāḥ mubāshiran/fa-mashīt li-mā an 'ata mutabakhtiran) (reproduced in as-Susi 1961: XIII, 171-172). After their meeting, Ahmad returned to Bzu. 'Abd ar-Rahman returned directly to Marrakesh to pack his belongings.

As his brother's unpaid deputy, 'Abd ar-Rahman's responsibilities were minimal. He attended all sessions of the court, held in his brother's house, and acted as overseer for the various lands in possession of his family. As Ahmad was almost never absent from court, 'Abd ar-Rahman first acted in the place of his brother only in December 1953, when his

---

[1] In speaking with me on general themes, 'Abd ar-Rahman was careful always to refer to non-Muslims by their nationality, and corrected members of his household when they employed the more popular usages of "Christian" (naṣrānī) and "Roman" (rūmī). In speaking of his own past, he used the terms he then employed.

[2] In 1950 Bu Naʿmani was appointed deputy (khalīfa) to Hajj Thami al-Glawi, although he lost this post after 1953 because he was a "neutral" who did not support the French deposition of the sultan that year. After independence in 1956 he became Pasha of Agadir, a post which he retained until the earthquake which destroyed much of the city in 1960.

brother was summarily transferred to the coastal city of aṣ-Ṣwīra (Mogador), where he served briefly as qadi until being removed from the post because of failure to support the French deposition of Sultan Sidi Muhammad bin Yusif.[3]

Once in Bzu, 'Abd ar-Rahman set about soliciting ijazas from his teachers in Marrakesh and men of learning of his acquaintance. Such documents had become devalued in urban milieus, but they still carried weight in rural settings. 'Abd ar-Rahman eventually acquired four ijazas, three from shaykhs at the Yusufiya, Mukhtar as-Susi, Muhammad bin 'Umar as-Sarghini, and Mulay Ahmad al-'Alami. The fourth he acquired in 1938, from the leader of the Kittaniya religious order in Fez, Shaykh 'Abd al-Ḥayy al-Kittānī.

These ijazas retain a profound meaning for 'Abd ar-Rahman. He copied by hand each of his letters requesting them, written in the flowery, rhymed prose similar to that of his speech defending Marrakesh, and preserved them carefully along with the documents he received. Since Mukhtar as-Susi was arrested by the French in 1935 and thereafter confined to his natal village in the Sus, signs of association with him might have been construed as incriminating in 1946 and 1953, the two times when 'Abd ar-Rahman destroyed many of his papers out of fear of imminent arrest by the French. Despite the danger involved, 'Abd ar-Rahman carefully preserved as-Susi's ijaza.

As-Susi used the ijazas he wrote for rural men of learning as vehicles to further his views on Islam and Moroccan society. Although the ijazas from 'Abd ar-Rahman's two other teachers adhered to earlier forms, listing the qualifications and education of the teacher and the texts studied with the student, as-Susi's ranged beyond these themes. His ijaza for 'Abd ar-Rahman is dated 2 Safar 1354/6 May 1935. It begins by saying that the entire world is changing except for Morocco, which remains in ignorance. Fez and Marrakesh, he wrote, are still

---

[3] Because he also declined to support the new sultan, 'Abd ar-Rahman was also removed from his brief tenure as qadi of Bzu on April 28, 1954.

asleep, and the men of learning are dying one by one. Religious learning by itself no longer suffices to maintain a sound society. After this unconventional prelude, as-Susi describes the circumstances of his own life. He relates that his father died in 1328/1910-1911, before he completed memorizing the Quran, and he describes his studies at various madrasas in southern Morocco, the continuation of his studies under Bu Shu'ayb and other scholars during his first stay at the Yusufiya (1919-1923), subsequent studies at the Qarawiyin at the time of the Riffian revolt (1923-1927), subsequent travels, and his return to teach at the Yusufiya in 1929. His style is lively and intimate, even when adhering to the contours of the traditional ijaza. He shapes the genre to his own sense of learning rather than merely perpetuating a received literary form. Although as-Susi uses the third person characteristic of such documents, he infuses the ijaza with personal opinion and reflection. By according similar documents to other rural students attracted by his ideas, he propagated his vision of reformist Islam into Morocco's smaller towns and villages, an elusive task for most reformists.

As-Susi does not enumerate the books he commented upon when 'Abd ar-Rahman attended his lesson circles. Such enumerations are, in fact, rare for ijazas written in the 1930s. Due to his frequent travels, his lesson circles were in any case only irregularly offered in Marrakesh. Instead, he lists the subjects studied: grammar, jurisprudence, rhetoric, literature, history, the sayings and actions of the Prophet, and Quranic exegesis. This range of subjects was far beyond the more limited scope offered by most men of learning. As-Susi's conclusion is unique, for he writes that 'Abd ar-Rahman is not his student, but his brother. He used similar language in other ijazas.

'Abd ar-Rahman's ijaza from 'Abd al-Hayy is quite different. It is dated 19 Rajab 1357/14 September 1938, when 'Abd al-Hayy was at the end of a week-long stay in Bzu as part of a protectorate-approved circuit throughout rural Morocco in order to collect donations for his religious activities. Shaykh 'Abd al-Hayy was then at the height of his powers. A distinguished scholar who also enjoyed considerable popular support, he was also known to be quietly antagonistic to the 'Alawi dynasty. His opposition to political movements brought him further favor with protectorate authorities, who accorded him privileges they withheld from other religious leaders. His downfall came in the 1950s, when he was one of the principal leaders of the movement leading to the deposition of Sidi Muhammad bin Yusif. In the 1930s, however, his friendship was still desirable. Shortly after his visit to Bzu, he was instrumental in securing admission of 'Abd ar-Rahman's half-brother, 'Abd al-Hayy, to the Qarawiyin (see Chapter Two).

'Abd ar-Rahman's ijaza from 'Abd al-Hayy al-Kittani represents a breakthrough in the vulgarization of the genre. It was a printed form with blank lines for the date, the name of the supplicant, and the books "studied." Rather than certify the transmission of a designated body of learning from one generation of scholars to another, it took more the form of a certificate of attendance at a lecture by the shaykh. Each night during the shaykh's stay in Bzu, between the sunset and evening prayers, 'Abd al-Hayy commented on al-Bukhari's collection of the sayings of the Prophet. 'Abd ar-Rahman acted as his reader.

'Abd al-Hayy's direct contact with 'Abd ar-Rahman was thus minimal. He had only visited Bzu once before, and 'Abd ar-Rahman saw him face to face only twice again. An avid bibliophile, the shaykh visited Bzu again in January 1944, where he remained as a guest of Qadi Ahmad while visiting the nearby zawiya of Ait Umghār and the shrine of Mulay Ḥusayn, a claimed ancestor of the Kittanis. Another reason for the visit was to inspect the manuscripts of the zawiya of Tamanghilt, also close to Bzu. Qadi Ahmad doubled locally as overseer of pious endowments, so he was in a position to oblige the zawiya to allow the inspection of its holdings; he dutifully led 'Abd al-Hayy there with other men of learning assembled for the purpose. The final occasion was in Fez, where 'Abd ar-Rahman and his friend, Hasan al-Bu Na'mani, visited the shaykh's house in 1944.

'Abd ar-Rahman proudly identifies himself as a carrier of reformist thought and is skeptical of religious brotherhoods. Yet he respected 'Abd al-Hayy sufficiently to seek an ijaza from him. His subsequent ambivalence toward 'Abd al-Hayy, discussed below, suggests both an implicit realization of the practical constraints upon men of learning in a rural context and 'Abd ar-Rahman's own emerging intellectual and political maturity.

Discerning Islam

Like their urban counterparts, men of learning in rural Morocco were aware of the major intellectual and political movements of their generation. At the same time, they were firmly enmeshed in local politics and society, where prevalent conceptions of Islamic belief and practice were not in accord with either reformist thought or entrenched interests. As unchanging as the image of formal religious learning was to some French observers of the colonial era, this learning was undergoing major internal debate and challenge.[4] This was also the case for more "popular" understandings of Islamic belief and practice (Eickelman 1976). As 'Abd ar-Rahman matured, his conceptions of Islam underwent transformations that were mirrored in the experiences of many other men of learning in rural Morocco.

In the 1920s and early 1930s, in Morocco as in neighboring Algeria (Merad 1967: 58-76), reformists saw major threats to Islam in the prevailing participation in religious brotherhoods and in various maraboutic practices, which are based upon the belief that certain persons, living or dead, have a special relation to God that makes them particularly well

---

[4] One of the few colonial observers aware of the significance of these debates was Jacques Berque. See Berque (1974: 162-188) for an excellent discussion, based upon his contemporary notes and discussions with the principals, of the concerns of religious intellectuals in the 1930s.

placed to serve as intermediaries with the supernatural and to communicate God's grace (baraka) to their clients.

Although reformist Islam received limited support in Morocco in the early nineteenth century (Abun-Nasr 1963), by the late nineteenth century it had emerged as a major influence among Morocco's religious intelligentsia and received the support of a succession of sultans. In Marrakesh, reformist thought was promoted by influential advocates, including Bu Shu'ayb ad-Dukkali, his student Mukhtar as-Susi, and Muhammad ibn 'Uthmān.[5] Because Marrakesh was under the heavy hand of Hajj Thami al-Glawi, the fusion of reformist thought and nationalist politics that was taking place in Fez in the early 1930s was less publicly apparent in Marrakesh. In Fez, men such as 'Allal al-Fassi could form a bridge between the traditional world of learning (he lectured at the Qarawiyin) and the early nationalist movement (al-Fassi 1954: 111-136). Nonetheless, no significant obstacles were placed to the spread of reformist doctrines, so long as their advocates refrained from endorsing nationalist aspirations. Many rural students at the Yusufiya were strongly influenced by reformist Islam and carried the lessons of their shaykhs back to their small towns and villages of origin, where they were confronted daily with the contrasts between reformist teachings and prevalent local understandings of Islam. As-Susi and ad-Dukkali, themselves of rural origin, were especially aware of the importance of disseminating reformist thought in rural areas, and kept regular contact with former students throughout the region by far-flung networks of patronage and influence.

Through studies at the Yusufiya, 'Abd ar-Rahman became caught up in the reformist movement. At the same time, as the son of a tribal notable and landowner and younger brother

[5] A leading figure at the Yusufiya during the 1930s who was recognized by the French as "rector" (ra'īs) of the Yusufiya from 1941 until his death in March 1944. He is the author of a history of the Yusufiya ('Uthman 1935), printed in Cairo, which unfortunately stops before the nineteenth century.

of an influential judge, he was aware of the political and economic realities of rural Morocco. In 1976 he recalled:

> Until I went to the Yusufiya, I thought that the religious brotherhoods were a part of Islam. In my studies, I read commentaries against the brotherhoods. I began to realize that even the practices of my father were not part of Islam. By the time I left the Yusufiya, I knew that the brotherhoods were an error.

When he first arrived at the Yusufiya, 'Abd ar-Rahman was himself drawn to one of the religious orders. Many Makhzan officials were members of the Tijani order. He attended some of their meetings and read their literature. What stuck most in his memory was their practice of wearing a shawl (*lizār*) when reciting the litany (*wird*) of the order. After a member's death, the Tijani shawl doubled as his shroud. For 'Abd ar-Rahman, the symbolic use of such a material object was highly suspect and therefore to be avoided.

For 'Abd ar-Rahman, some religious orders are more in violation of authentic Islamic practices than others, and must be explained in historical context. His father, he explained, distanced himself from a number of practices almost universal in his generation, such as visits (*ziyāra*s) to maraboutic shrines and the reading of books of the miraculous deeds of maraboutic figures. The Kittani religious order, like the Tijani, attracted adherents from the sultan's entourage in the early twentieth century. He did not use the dismissive tone for these orders that he reserved for comment on the less exclusive ones. In any case, before and during the protectorate era, Morocco's rulers gave the leaders of religious orders decrees of investiture, providing them with a cachet of approval. Nonetheless, after his studies at the Yusufiya, 'Abd ar-Rahman decided that all religious orders deviated to some degree from authentic Islamic practice. He explained his personal opposition to religious brotherhoods by elaborating on the distinction between the path of Islam (*ash-shrā'*), a term that encompasses both formal Islamic law and accepted Islamic practice, and innovation (bid'a), for which there is no Islamic precedent. This distinction is integrally related to his sense of history and personal responsibility.

To clarify the distinction, 'Abd ar-Rahman drew two parallel lines on a sheet of paper. He explained that everything within the lines was shra', the path constituted by the Quran and the words and deeds of the Prophet Muhammad, as they are interpreted by Islamic jurists. All other practice—and here he indicated the boundless space outside of his parallel lines—was bid'a, beyond the pale of Islamic conduct. He further explained that some practices were outside the path of Islam but not directly opposed to it. He penciled a line just outside one of the two parallel lines. He used this notion to explain legislative innovations not contained in Islamic law and the varying degrees to which the practices of religious brotherhoods constituted innovation.

In this conception of Islam, the advice of men of learning distinguished by their knowledge of the religious sciences and "the way things are done" (al-qā'ida) is essential to delineate authoritatively authentic Islamic practice. Such persons 'Abd ar-Rahman refers to collectively as the elite (nas khassa). They are distinguished by an ability to discern between shra' and bid'a. Other persons, even if they are of high political rank, are commoners ('awam). Those informed by a proper sense of the path of Islam are less likely to be taken in by confidence men (dajjāla) from religious orders or maraboutic shrines, and to be aware of the fundamental precepts of Islamic law governing marriage contracts and inheritance settlements. It is in any case the duty of a Muslim is to seek authoritative advice.

The distinction is not between urban and rural society, although he argues that persons in the country are less likely to have a clear understanding of Islamic practice. To illustrate his argument, he asked me to consider the courtroom comportment of persons of rural origin. In the courtroom, many tribesmen and women have difficulty in explaining the facts of their case in an appropriate form. Their descriptions of incidents are tied to highly local knowledge and they are often unable to describe the timing and duration of events in the abstract, datable form necessary for the application of Islamic law (Davis 1983: 95-97). Compared to town-dwellers, rural persons are less able to perform such a "translation" from locally comprehended descriptions of events, and lack a clear understanding of the specific requirements of Islamic law.

For 'Abd ar-Rahman, bid'a exists historically. Before Islam, no one was capable of living by the shra' because it was not yet revealed, so that everything was bid'a. Consider, he explained, the state of mystical exaltation (*ḥāl*), for which some participants in religious orders work themselves into a trance (*jadba*). He explained that this is a vestige of the time of Sidna Musa (Moses), the prophet "who came before Muhammad offered mankind the keys to the mosque." After Islam, some people added to Islam practices that do not exist within Islam itself. Muhammad came as the "seal" of the prophets, so that actions attributed to him carry a validity above that of the other prophets, and to which nothing further can be added. Yet the practices that preceded the coming of the Prophet have not disappeared, so the problem remains of how to reconcile them with Islam. He provided as an example the issue of saints (*wālīs*) in Islam.

> Commoners are ignorant (*juhhāl*). Many of them do not know what Islam is, and what their ancestors did. So someone can tell them a story of the miracles of a marabout and they will be happy.

Only the prophets, including Muhammad and his predecessors, can perform miracles. But there have been men since the time of the prophet Muhammad who are blessed (*'andhum karāma*) in the sense that they are used as instruments of God's will. The naive and the gullible in Morocco attribute miraculous powers to certain marabouts, persons whom men of learning regard as distinguished only by piety, lineage, and scholarship. He dismissed the miracle-working powers attributed to Sharqawi marabouts with a wave of his hand.

To 'Abd ar-Rahman, men of learning are also distinguished

from other Muslims through possession of a sense of history that encompasses a knowledge of genealogies (*ḥasab wa-na-sab*)(see K. Brown 1972: 131), prior rulers and dynasties, and key Islamic events. Although history (*ta'rīkh*) refers broadly to a knowledge of all past events and an ability to place them in their proper context, the illustrations upon which Hajj 'Abd ar-Rahman constantly drew concerned the immediate antecedents of men of power and learning. Knowledge of their genealogies, intermarriages, economic interests, and antagonisms rendered contemporary social action more predictable. Thus he characterized 'Abd al-Hayy al-Kittani, a religious leader with whose conduct he disagreed strongly, in the following terms:

> He was a great man of learning (*'ālim kbīr*). There were few like him in all the Maghrib. His library was one of the finest in the country. He could talk to a man and know everything about him: the name of his father, his grandfather, his ancestors, his brothers. Likewise he knew the history of everyone in the Maghrib.

Along the same lines, the first entries in 'Abd ar-Rahman's notebooks after he arrived in Boujad in 1957 are copies of sections of court documents related to Sharqawi kinship relations and property. Such history was directly useful in dealing knowledgeably with persons of influence.

Access to such historical knowledge is most readily available to the elite, who are better qualified to obtain knowledge through chains of reliable, known witnesses. Important knowledge, especially of political events, is often passed only by word of mouth among trusted confidants, signaling its exclusive nature. 'Abd ar-Rahman explained that the chronicles of kings and the actions of their key ministers were often deliberately obscure in written sources. Everyone is afraid to write of such events. But the oral tradition available to men of learning provides the background necessary to understand events and their significance. Commoners lack access to such knowledge and the ability to assess its veracity.

As an example of such historical knowledge, 'Abd ar-Rah-man explained to me how he first learned of the militant antagonism of 'Abd al-Hayy al-Kittani to the 'Alawi dynasty.[6]

I heard this [in the 1930s] from an ex-slave of Mulay 'Abd al-Hafid [r. 1908-1912], 'Abd al-Bāqī. Before becoming a slave of the sultan, he was a slave at the zawiya of Sidi Muḥammad bin Nāṣir in Tanaghmilt (Ntifa). Mu-ḥammad bin 'Abd al-Kabīr al-Kittānī ad-Drīsī was head of the Qarawiyin [and of the Kittaniya order]. He refused to give the oath of allegiance to Mulay 'Abd al-Hafid unless the sultan agreed to certain conditions. The sultan was angered. 'Abd al-Kabir fled, together with his wives, family, and servants to the Bnī Mgīld, a tribe which was then out of reach of the Makhzan and loyal to the Kit-taniyin shurfa.[7] Before he fled from Fez, 'Abd al-Kabir sent a rosary [tasbīḥ] and a copy of the Quran to the sultan, the traditional tokens for requesting a pardon. The sultan had the slave who carried the message buried alive at night, together with the gifts, so that no one [except presumably the slaves such as 'Abd al-Baqi who were entrusted with the task] would know that al-Kittani ever sought a pardon.

A document prepared by 'Abd ar-Rahman just after he was appointed qadi of Boujad (May 6, 1957) gives a practical indication of whom he considered to be men of learning. Since his appointment obliged him to leave Bzu indefinitely—in-

---

[6] Kittani hostility to the 'Alawi dynasty culminated in 'Abd al-Hayy's active collaboration in colonial efforts to discredit Muhammad bin Yusif and support Mulay 'Arafa, the "puppet" sultan enthroned by the French after Muhammad bin Yusif's exile to Madagascar in 1953.

[7] 'Abd ar-Rahman here telescopes a complex series of events. In March 1909, to discourage rebellion during his absence in Marrakesh, Sultan Mulay 'Abd al-Hafid intended to secure several Fassi notables as hostages. When news of the sultan's intentions reached Muhammad al-Kittani on March 19, he secretly fled to the Middle Atlas mountains. He was eventually brought back to Fez, where he later died from beatings he received in prison (see Burke 1976: 133-134).

deed, he subsequently chose to retire in Boujad—he was aware that an era had come to an end. He prepared a list of men of learning who had been entertained at his brother's house in Bzu from its construction in the 1920s until Morocco's independence. The heading of the list specifies " *'ulamā' wa-shu-rafā'*," but only those shurfa who were also men of learning are included. Most visits occurred in the 1930s, the apogee of the colonial period.

'Abd ar-Rahman's list encompassed 130 individuals, all of whom he also described as nas khassa, the learned elite. His list included the leaders of two key religious orders—religious orders retained popular respect in Morocco until the postwar rise of mass nationalism—urban and rural judges, high officials of the Ministry of Justice, a few educated shurfa, teachers at the Qarawiyin and Yusifiya mosque-universities, traditionally educated tutors of the children of Hajj Thami al-Glawi and the royal family, and several urban merchants and pashas (political administrators of principal towns). Most persons on the list were at least moderately wealthy, although there were exceptions. It included an itinerant Sufi (*majdūb*), dressed in rags, reputed throughout southern Morocco with mystical insight although he never uttered a word. He was assured hospitality at the houses of men of learning throughout southern Morocco. Other exceptions were some of the teachers at the two mosque-universities. Islamic learning had provided them with a means of social mobility. Jewish men of learning, like the French, were not enumerated, although 'Abd ar-Rahman recalls that one of his elder brother's respected local friends was a rabbi in Bzu who visited him regularly.

I asked a man of learning who was a contemporary of 'Abd ar-Rahman but from Marrakesh to evaluate the names on his list. His assessment of who were "really" men of learning was much more restricted than 'Abd ar-Rahman's. He dismissed a number of qadis and clerks in the protectorate's Ministry of Justice as "mere functionaries" who had no more than a rudimentary understanding of the religious sciences. Despite disagreement as to who properly qualified as men of learning, the scholar from Marrakesh used the same implicit criteria as 'Abd ar-Rahman: a demonstrated command of Islamic knowledge and its acquisition from men previously recognized as men of learning themselves.

SELF-IMAGES

When he first visited Bzu, Hasan al-Bu Na'mani wrote a long, vivid letter to Mukhtar as-Susi, then in forced residence in Iligh, his natal village in the Sus. The letter, dated 14 Jumada 1355/2 August 1936 (reproduced in as-Susi 1961: XIII, 174-180), was recited to his hosts before his departure. The letter offers vivid insight into the self-image of men of learning, an issue implicit in 'Abd ar-Rahman's careful inventory of learned visitors to Bzu. In his letter, Bu Na'mani writes ironically of France's protectorate as the "brotherly dictatorship" (al-diktāturīya al-ikhā'iya) (as-Susi 1961: XIII, 180). The letter alludes to politics, but politics is not its central concern. It is a mixture of circumstantial detail and exuberant literary allusion, so that its audience is self-consciously confined to those who share an awareness of valued literary texts, just as men of learning "possessed" common religious texts.

Bu Na'mani writes that as soon as he stepped off the bus at the Wad al-'Abid bridge, where the track to Bzu joined the motor road, he was approached by a servant leading a "superb" riding mule. Indeed, he claims hyperbolically that the servant and the mule were both so distinguished in appearance that they attracted the attention of bystanders gathered at the banks of the river. Later, as he approached "fragrant" Bzu, he discerned villagers standing on a small promontory overlooking the path, with the women ululating in pleasure at his arrival. He finally arrived at the house of Qadi Ahmad, which was also the law court. "Sidi"[8] 'Abd ar-Rahman, the respected

---

[8] *Sīdī* is an honorific generally reserved for royalty and prominent marabouts. Bu Na'mani here deliberately uses it to elevate 'Abd ar-Rahman in status. The ordinary term of address would be *Sī*.

man of letters, waited for him at the door, surrounded by retainers, assistants, relatives, and a crowd of litigants. "Happiness and pleasure overflowed on their faces." After saying "in the name of God" at the threshhold, Bu Na'mani and the group entered the elegant garden of Qadi Ahmad's courtyard. It was "as fragrant as a garden of paradise." Bu Na'mani assures his audience that even the birds broke out in song for the occasion.

"Then as a sign of great happiness, court was suspended for the day and the litigants dispersed. We devoted ourselves wholeheartedly to pleasures and conversed delightfully on whatever pleased us." The "us" in Bu Na'mani's narrative presumably excluded the litigants, who may not have been entirely overjoyed at having their concerns abruptly set aside in honor of a young poet from Marrakesh. Bu Na'mani's "us" also refers implicitly to the elite, in this case formed by men of learning, as opposed to commoners. Citing lines from contemporary Moroccan poets and those of earlier generations, Bu Na'mani narrates that the abundance of literary allusions raised in their meeting "almost swept away dignified bearing" on the part of those present, so intoxicated were they with the occasion. It was the sort of occasion where "brotherhood and forthrightness prevail . . . in which princes forget their responsibilities and their dignified countenance before the world, and the modest man of letters forgets his reserve."

Bu Na'mani's letter includes a description of the food he was served, the verses he composed in praise of Bzu during his stay, and the entire letter in which 'Abd ar-Rahman initially invited him to Bzu. He comments of this letter that anyone reading it would immediately think that it was written by a man of letters from Muslim Cordoba in a playful mood. As for Bzu, Bu Na'mani avers that its beauty, graced by the presence of 'Abd ar-Rahman and his cultured elder brother, made him forget even Marrakesh. Despite its hyperbole, the letter also conveys informality. Bu Na'mani even alludes to a concubine provided for his stay (as-Susi 1961: XIII, 180).

The letter's style is self-consciously what Moroccans today

call "Egyptian writing," a style specific to the literary ren-
naissance (*nahḍa*) and proliferation of small literary magazines in Morocco during the 1930s.[9] Although this style bears
no inherent correlation to reformist Islam, it was introduced
primarily by men of learning influenced by Egyptian thought.
This "new literature" (*al-adab al-jadīd*), a term used by as-
Susi (1961: XIII, 174) to characterize Bu Naʻmani's letter, is
distinguished by references to classical Arabic poetry, especially that of Muslim Spain, and by frequent reference to
books and manuscripts by other men of learning.

Men such as Bu Naʻmani were in some respects "hired
guns," to adapt Schumpeter's (1962: 147-148) description of
medieval European intellectuals whose fortunes were closely
attached to those of their patrons. Bu Naʻmani was not independently wealthy and lived off his wits. Like other men of
learning in his condition, the occasional poems and letters he
wrote while making the rounds of rural notables were recom-
pensed with presents and lavish hospitality. Letters were his
precarious métier. Others made the rounds of men of learning
to secure institutional funds. Madani bin Husni, director of
the Free School (*madrasa ḥurra*) in Marrakesh, an "independent" school established by urban merchants and other
Muslims concerned with creating an Islamic alternative to
colonial schooling (see Damis 1974), also travelled regularly
to rural notables to collect funds for his school. Such visitors
enhanced the reputations of rural hosts.

BZU: THE TWO FACES OF LEARNING

Successful comportment as a notable involved maintaining a
delicate balance between competing pressures: competition
from other notables, local supporters, the sultan's entourage,
and the French administration. Because Bzu remained a region
without significant colonization, the Islamic law court continued to be the primary vehicle for the resolution of land

---

[9] I am grateful to Muhammad Aafif for explaining to me the implications
of this style of writing in Morocco.

disputes for all lands except those considered "tribal," which fell directly under the jurisdiction of French authorities. In outlying rural regions, some inheritance and land disputes were resolved without recourse to the courts, although an aggrieved party in an extra-court settlement could always later exercise the option of formally initiating a claim in court.

In a rural setting such as Bzu, there was a constant interplay between a knowledge of the formalities of Islamic law and an understanding of the limits of what could be accomplished in any given context. The Mansuri brothers were credited with a knowledge of the precepts of Islamic law and of accepted local practice (al-qā'ida), together with the "social rationality" or "reason" ('qāl) to resolve disputes equitably. Hence the work of qadi was conducted on two levels, that of Islamic law and that of local understandings of what was right and just. A qadi was not just a functionary, as he has too often become in contemporary Morocco; his sound knowledge of the law was combined with an understanding of local society. Quite often much of the work of the qadi consisted in advising persons on how to conduct themselves in accord with the precepts of Islam so as to avoid resolution of their disputes in court. Continuing the tradition of their father, the Mansuri brothers were respected for their willingness out of court to help their clients reconcile what they considered their rights with what was accorded them by Islamic law.

As carriers of religious knowledge, respected by men of learning and by persons in political authority, the Mansuris were treated with deference in Bzu. They were also respected as landowners and local functionaries. In the 1930s, as in preceding decades, marriage continued to be an important means for cementing political bonds. Qadi Ahmad's first marriage in the early 1920s was to the daughter of a local tribal shaykh and landowner. His second marriage in 1353/1934-1935 was to a daughter of the qaid of Ntifa, the same one with whom Ahmad's father had a serious dispute a decade earlier (see Chapter Two). In 1941, at the suggestion of his elder brother, 'Abd ar-Rahman further solidified this tie by marrying another daughter of the same qaid. These links provided

FIGURE 3. 'Abd ar-Rahman, 1939.

the Mansuri brothers with the outside support they needed to maintain their local preeminence.

The Mansuri brothers were wealthy by the standards of the Marrakesh hinterland, but not extragavantly so. By the late 1930s they had acquired roughly 400 hectares (988 acres) of land and sizable livestock herds. They introduced mechanized agriculture and motor pumps for irrigation to some of their fields, and possessed two automobiles.

A major advantage of being considered among the "known people" (*nās maʿrūfīn*) was a greater security of property. Title to lands in much of the Bzu region was by *rasm*, written agreement between buyer and seller drawn up in accordance with the tenets of Islamic law. The land involved in such transactions was often specified by local names, with actual boundaries known to members of the community rather than formally specified. When disputes over the actual limits of such land occurred, they could be resolved only by persons already familiar with the parcels of land in question and the validity of the claims of documents and witnesses to the land in question. In adjudicating such disputes, judges relied inevitably upon the word of shaykhs and local notables. In the Bzu region itself, Qadi Ahmad was clearly the ultimate arbiter.

Unlike other parts of Morocco, virtually no land around Bzu was registered by the Torrens system of land registration, introduced by colonial authorities. Under the Torrens system, persons wishing to claim title to a plot of land register their claim, which is then surveyed to determine precise boundaries. Official notice is then given of the claim. Prior or conflicting documents are examined to evaluate their validity. All documents are registered in one central place, so that a single search reveals the status of a title. Registration of land under the Torrens system is known among Moroccan notables as possession by *titre*: the French term is used. In principle, possession of a Torrens title greatly reduced the possibility of boundary disputes. Yet as 'Abd ar-Rahman pointed out, notables rarely needed such protection. In fact, there was a clear disadvantage to holding a Torrens title, for it left no ambiguity over the extent of holdings for taxation purposes. Official French reports gave the extent of the Mansuri family's property at roughly half of what they actually possessed. Such ambiguity was an unintended advantage of maintaining title whenever possible under Islamic law.

Prestige and authority exist to the extent that they are publicly displayed and reaffirmed. The attention given by rural notables to attending wedding feasts, funerals, and other significant gatherings of notables served not only to confirm patterns of practical domination, but sought to reaffirm it to outsiders. As 'Abd ar-Rahman explained, having a constant flow of visitors to one's house and visiting notables elsewhere lets one know what is going on in the world. The search for information and ability to obtain and recognize firm "news" (C. Geertz 1979: 198-212) is facilitated when one is a notable. Whenever decisions had to be made affecting Bzu, the Mansuris were consulted and their advice heeded. Through regular patterns of reciprocal visiting, notables became apprised of one another's interests and the practical limits of what was possible in current political situations. By the late 1930s and early 1940s, 'Abd ar-Rahman began visiting other urban centers and rural notables on his own, at times in the company of his friend, Hasan al-Bu Na'mani.

A sense of the scale and importance of such feasting is provided by the marriages of Ahmad in the mid-1930s and 'Abd ar-Rahman in 1941. For Ahmad's wedding, 'Abd ar-Rahman recorded the name of each prominent guest, together with the present given to each of them, a varying mixture of cash and locally made Bziwi jallabas. The guests included qaids, qadis and their deputies from the regions adjoining Bzu; the deputy pasha of Marrakesh, Captain Ben Daoud, an Algerian-born military interpreter who was also editor of the protectorate newspaper, as-Sa'āda ("Happiness") (distributed free by colonial authorities to all persons designated as notables, and hence itself a minor indicum of status); several members of the Glawi family (although not the pasha himself); teachers from the Yusufiya; and key officials in the Ministry of Justice. 'Abd al-Hayy al-Kittani and Bu Shu'ayb ad-Dukkali both declined invitations to attend, but were nonetheless sent gifts, one jallaba for ad-Dukkali and three for al-Kittani. The total expense for the wedding was carefully recorded as 5,644 Hassani ryals. French colonial authorities and local Jewish notables were also present, although 'Abd ar-Rahman did not record their names. Nine thousand ryals were spent on a 1937 visit by 'Abd al-Hayy al-Kittani, and 160,000 for a visit of Sultan Muhammad bin Yusif to nearby Tamghalt, a visit hosted by the Mansuri brothers, in 1950.

'Abd ar-Rahman's own wedding is carefully reported in

articles that appeared in issues 5,429 and 5,430 of *as-Sa'ada*, dated December 27 and December 28, 1941. The categories of notables attending the wedding and the geographical range of invitees parallel those present at the wedding of his elder brother. *As-Sa'ada* reported that wedding guests were entertained throughout a month. The newspaper estimated that food for the wedding guests was provided through the slaughter of 800 sheep and 300-400 cows. These indications of scale are perhaps more significant than attempts to assign specific monetary value to the proceedings.

As an example of how the Mansuri brothers used their ties with other notables to defend their interests, a serious conflict developed between Qadi Ahmad and a new official appointed as overseer for pious endowments.[10] Shortly after being appointed qadi of Bzu in 1926, Ahmad Mansuri was given the additional appointment of overseer of pious endowments for the Bzu region. His letters of investiture from Sultan Mulay Yusuf (r. 1912-1927) for both posts were renewed when Sidi Muhammad bin Yusif assumed the throne in 1927. Ahmad continued to hold both posts until 1943, when the colonial government decided that henceforth no official could hold two posts simultaneously. This move coincided with a long-delayed implementation of an earlier reorganization of pious endowment administration in the region. A single overseer was appointed with responsibilities for the entire region of Marrakesh and Ntifa. Unlike his illiterate predecessor, the new overseer was literate and reasonably effective, and actually secured support for extending his effective control over the hinterland of Marrakesh. Qadi Ahmad remained as deputy overseer for the Bzu region, an unpaid position. Former overseers in other regions, often qadis, likewise continued as unpaid deputies.

The new overseer, from an influential family in Marrakesh,

[10] This account is based upon a narrative written by 'Abd ar-Rahman dated March 29, 1945, with supplementary verbal commentary provided in July 1976.

at first had the support of Qadi Ahmad. According to 'Abd ar-Rahman, when the new overseer was first appointed the Mansuri brothers considered him to be "close" to the sultan, in the sense of being in his favor. The man dressed poorly to indicate his humility and lack of avarice, and was himself considered to be a man of learning. Soon after his appointment, however, 'Abd ar-Rahman claimed that he began to exploit his office for personal gain.

In 1942 Qadi Ahmad acquired land in Marrakesh. On part of this land he constructed a *funduq*, an all-purpose caravanserai used for merchants' stalls, stored goods, stables, and, in this case, rooms for religious students. Its construction was completed in 1944. The overseer decided that he wanted to acquire Qadi Ahmad's Marrakesh property for himself. The land does not appear have fallen within his official jurisdiction, despite the fact that Qadi Ahmad allowed the hostel to be used in part to lodge religious students. He successfully acquired the land and the funduq. From the point of view of the Mansuri brothers, this was because he was supported by the French administration, with which the Mansuris were beginning to have difficulties. The dispute flared into the open and lasted for two years. After complicated maneuvers involving multiple intermediaries, this dispute and other outstanding ones were finally resolved in 1946 by Hajj Thami al-Glawi in the course of a personal visit to Bzu, during which he, of course, had to be suitably entertained. Qadi Ahmad failed to recover his lands in Marrakesh, but the pasha brought an end to the harrassment of the Mansuri brothers by local French officials, an objective that by then was more significant than lost property in Marrakesh.

THE RESPONSIBILITIES OF LEARNING

If a man of learning stands out because of his better knowledge of the straight path of Islam and of the skills needed to discern this path, I asked 'Abd ar-Rahman, then what is his responsibility toward his fellow Muslims? His reply was a paean to personal autonomy:

> A Muslim's duty is just to show the path to those who want to be with God, and that is that. Either they take it or leave it. The prophets allow them the choice. There is paradise and there is hell, and God selects who goes to each (see also Eickelman 1976: 126-130).

'Abd ar-Rahman's notion of responsibility focuses upon the social rationality of individuals regardless of economic class, their ability to discern their status and to act realistically in the context of contemporary society. As pointed out in Islamic contexts elsewhere (e.g., Kessler 1978: 211), such a notion of responsibility is profoundly asocial in the sense that the Islamic ideal is to be realized through individuals each improving his own conduct. There is no clear sense of collective goals short of those to be realized by the entire Islamic community. Such a conception of responsibility does not lend itself to a direct or central involvement in politics, although 'Abd ar-Rahman recognized that the political context in which the shra' is realized is important, if only because political authorities, both in the colonial era and subsequent to it, have had the capacity to thwart Islamic practice.

Even within the sphere of "nonpolitical" Islamic practice, the responsibilities of men of learning are circumscribed. 'Abd ar-Rahman described his only direct confrontation with 'Abd al-Hayy al-Kittani:

> In 1944 I went with my father to a big reunion of the Kittaniya in Fez. Followers came from all over the Maghrib—Tunisia, Algeria, and Morocco. Many of them were beating themselves, like my father did, and some went into trance. I said nothing. After all, my father and I were guests in the house of Shaykh 'Abd al-Hayy and most of the people there were under his authority (imra).

> Finally, although I was the shaykh's guest, I said to him that I had read an account of the orders which argued

that the very practices I had seen that day in Fez were bid'a, beyond the limits of Islamic conduct. 'Abd al-Hayy replied: "No. These practices help people to remain on the path of Islam." I replied: "Tell me [how]" ('allimnī). The shaykh did not reply. We did not return again to the subject.

'Abd ar-Rahman's direct challenge to the shaykh was contained in the public utterance of precisely one word, 'allimnī. I raised the question of why he did not further pursue the issue if he felt so strongly about the pernicious influence of brotherhoods. He replied that both he and Shaykh 'Abd al-Hayy were aware of their entrenched and divergent views. 'Abd ar-Rahman was moreover aware of the vastly superior status of the shaykh. Direct confrontation would have accomplished nothing. A futile display of anger or a persistent attempt to persuade a person irrevocably committed to a course of action to change his mind would display a lack of "reason" in the social arena. "Reasonable" men do not stand on absolute rights and wrongs. They seek to discern accurately the contours of existing social and political realities and on this basis calculate an effective course of action (see Eickelman 1976: 130-138).

In 'Abd ar-Rahman's view, there was also ample precedent for men of learning to cooperate with political authorities, even if they were French, provided that the wishes of the sultan and the principles of Islam were respected.

There is a saying of the prophet that we must obey God, the Prophet, and persons of authority (ahl al-amr). Ahl al-amr here in Morocco means the sultan.[11] So if the sultan decrees something which is not in the shra', I must nonetheless judge by it.

I then asked 'Abd ar-Rahman whether he felt that some of the laws by which he conducted his court were therefore bid'a.

[11] Like other men of his generation, 'Abd ar-Rahman frequently interchanges the terms "sultan" and "king."

The sultan does not issue decrees on his own. He tells us that the decree prohibiting the division of inherited lands below a certain size is in the interests (*maṣlaḥa*) of promoting agricultural development. He also decrees that according to doctors it is not good for women to have children before they are fifteen because they are not yet ready. I married my wife when she was thirteen, well before the new decree, and her first two children died. So perhaps what the doctors say is true. Still, some women can have babies early. I heard on the news yesterday that a nine-year old American girl gave birth, but doctors say that most women cannot. So our decree says that if a woman does not get a paper from the doctor saying that she is at least fifteen years old, a judge cannot declare her marriage valid. It is in the interest of the woman that the decree is made.

Moreover, when the sultan issues a decree, first he consults with fifteen or twenty men of learning. So if the sultan wants a decree which is against the principles (*qawā'id*) of Islam, he cannot get it because he will find no men of learning willing to say that the decree is not contradictory to Islamic principles. So the sultan cannot issue decrees which are against Islamic law.

The sophistry of the ruler being unable to legislate against the shra' is arguable in practice. After all, some men of learning, including 'Abd al-Hayy al-Kittani, signed the Glawi's petition calling for the deposition of Sidi Muhammad bin Yusif in 1953. Yet there are cases in recent Moroccan history in which the interpretations of men of learning have been used to legitimate opposition to the express wishes of the ruler. The most dramatic case in recent Moroccan history was the opposition to the new Moroccan constitution by the scholar Mulay al-'Arabī al-'Alawī, a sharif, student of Bu Shu'ayb ad-Dukkali, and tutor to the nationalist leader 'Allal al-Fassi. He opposed the constitution's endorsement of primogeniture in dynastic succession and a legislative assembly (see Waterbury

1970: 44, 92). He was not successful, but his objections were given wide publicity by those opposed to the constitution.

For 'Abd ar-Rahman, the implementation of Islamic law, not Islamic law itself, changes to accommodate political realities. He and his brother were not men of authority (*sulṭa*) in the sense of themselves making explicit political decisions. In times of acute crisis under the French, they sought to influence the political conduct of others by withholding support, not by actively working against the colonial system. For precedent they frequently cited the conduct of the monarch himself. Beginning in the late 1940s, political activists in the Istiqlal and other parties labeled such persons as "mystics" (*ṣūfīs*), using the term in a context which implies that they remained aloof from political activism.

The nationalist claim that men of traditional learning were "mystics" or "non-rational" (Waterbury 1970: 92) in this sense is incorrect. 'Allal al-Fassi, for example, despite his years as a student and teacher at the Qarawiyin, had developed significant contacts with both French opposition parties and Moroccans familiar with European political ideas (al-Fassi 1954). Their political ideas often paralleled those of their European and colonial counterparts, although their goal became liberation from European rule. Traditional men of learning recognized the fact of European political and technological superiority and resented it. Their response, however, was to address what they considered to be the most basic issue facing the Islamic community, to recapture its former momentum toward progress through internal discipline and educational reform (Binsa'id 1983: 32-35). When traditional men of learning were directly challenged, as they were with the deposition of Sidi Muhammad bin Yusif in 1953, an act that stripped all pretense of legitimacy from French rule, they were capable of courageous action.

SIX

Politics and Religion:
From Protectorate to Independence

THE BERBER DECREE

Explicit political challenge to colonial rule began to crystallize in 1930. The challenge was initially formulated as a religious one. The Berber Decree formally extracted certain Berber-speaking areas of Morocco from the jurisdiction of Islamic courts, submitting disputes to customary law courts instead. The decree was issued on May 16, 1930. The first demonstration against it took place in Salé, Rabat's twin city, on June 20, 1930. Kenneth Brown's (1973) excellent account of the event, based in part upon interviews with participants, 'Abd ar-Rahman's contemporaries, makes it clear that the leadership was almost entirely in the hands of the sons of the town's elite, both those who were attending French schools and those with a traditional education. They shaped their protest in religious terms that won widespread popular support.

The protest took the form of public recitations of the *laṭīf*, a collective invocation to God in times of disaster or distress. The issue was framed as one of purification of the Muslim community, in this case from a disaster attributable to rule by non-Muslims, the Berber Decree. The latif was a form of public gathering understood by all generations of Moroccans. Soon other cities throughout Morocco followed the lead of Salé. Marrakesh was an exception. For 'Abd ar-Rahman, ignorance was to blame, although the fact that his brother warned him to stay away from imminent demonstrations for fear of arrest suggests an equal concern with political reprisals.

Few people in Marrakesh could then read or understand what the French were doing. Fez was burning with reaction to the proclamation. In Marrakesh, we read the newspapers [prohibited by the French], but did not know what they meant. The [Berber] proclamation was against the shra', but we didn't realize that at the time. Besides, the city was under the firm hand of the Glawi. Anyone who went against him risked certain imprisonment.

When I pressed him on why he did not seek to explain to people in Marrakesh the implications of the Berber Decree if indeed they were unaware that it was a threat against Islam, he replied that his primary concern was his religious studies, which participation in political activity could bring to a sudden end.

'Abd ar-Rahman nevertheless shared with the early nationalists the sentiment that Islam was threatened. Before he left for studies at the Yusufiya, he remembers once having visited a small, French-run school. He recalls the older boys at the school smoking, allowing their hair to grow, and knowing nothing of the Quran. "They had lost Islam." Despite Lyautey's earlier efforts to create an amalgam of French and Islamic education for notables, French educational efforts were regarded with mistrust. Colonial rule was an attack upon Islam, and it was in these terms that French rule was most readily understood. For many educated urban youth of his generation, the shift to proto-nationalist activities began in the early and mid-1930s. For 'Abd ar-Rahman this shift never took place, although he was intimately aware of nationalist activities and goals.

So long as the fiction of respect for Islam and the formal consent of the sultan could be maintained, the French had the acquiesence of most men of learning. Once that fiction began to crack in the late 1940s with a series of open confrontations between the Palace and the Residence, the days of French rule were numbered.

THE COLONIAL APOGÉE

Colonial rule unintentionally strengthened the networks linking educated rural notables. The size of rural administration during the colonial era was admittedly miniscule in comparison with the burgeoning bureaucracy of the postcolonial era, but it nonetheless provided a number of previously unavailable sinecures for the traditionally educated.

The French vision of rural Morocco was that of a honeycomb, with the notables within each cell jockeying over matters of local import (Montagne 1941: 19; Gellner 1973: 367-368). The French, by favoring what one intelligence officer called the "natural leaders" (Berriau 1918: 4-5) within each cell, supported those local notables whose interests could be made to articulate most closely with their own. In this French vision, the highest local Moroccan official, the qaid, would only communicate officially outside of his cell through a French Native Affairs Officer (ḥākim) or Civil Controller (murāqib), the lowest officials in the French native administrative hierarchy. Consequently all communications between the sultan and his appointed local officials were to be brokered through the French administration (Gellner 1973: 367-368).

French understanding of Moroccan rural society neglected the pervasive transregional ties of patronage and influence among notables and men of learning, which could be used to subvert the official French hierarchy. Rural notables easily remained abreast of major political developments throughout Morocco and the Islamic world, often obtained access to confidential French documents concerning themselves, and circulated banned newspapers with ease. Especially after relations between the sultan and the French deteriorated in the decade following the Second World War, local notables devised means of regular communication with the Palace that evaded French control.

In discussing the Mansuri brothers in the 1970s, some urban-born scholars in Marrakesh described them to me as modest country fqihs who like others of their kind owed their careers to collaboration with the French. Moroccan intellectuals, like others, are capable of judging past actions through the simplified prism of the present. The Mansuri brothers, together with many other men of learning of their generation, collaborated with the men of authority. In doing so, they followed the lead of their monarchs, a succession of whom accepted French "tutelage." When the ruler began increasingly to chart a course independent from that of the French, the Mansuri brothers continued to follow his lead, often displaying personal courage.

In 1962-1963, a schoolteacher from Tetouan, capital of Morocco's former Spanish zone and a center of learning, asked Qadi Ahmad to prepare a tarjama, so that his participation in the events of the early part of this century would be recorded in his own hand. Unlike many of his contemporaries, Qadi Ahmad did not rewrite his personal history to conform to contemporary fashion. It did not omit his role in organizing the first rural tax and the "pacification" of the Ait 'Tab, an act which in his view averted unnecessary bloodshed. The tarjama omits only the fact that he was awarded a colonial medal for his actions. It is admittedly somewhat self-serving in recounting how a local Native Affairs officer in 1953 recognized Qadi Ahmad's integrity and therefore successfully recommended against sending him to prison, the fate of many other notables courageous enough to refrain from publicly supporting the sultan's exile to Madagascar in 1953.

The tarjamas of many of Qadi Ahmad's contemporaries often downplay the significance of their involvement with the French. An example is provided in as-Susi's (1961: IX, 35-37) compendium of men of learning in the Sus. According to one entry, when in 1914 the French conquered the region in which Sidi Aḥmad al-Aḥrīyi al-Tajarmuntī (b. 1897) was teaching, they saw his excellence in spite of his youth. "Humbly and deferentially," the French invited Sidi Ahmad's cooperation. The tarjama then depicts a career in which the scholar first was obliged to assist the French in making a survey of land ownership in the region, then returned to religious teaching, a second interval of unspecified work for the French, and finally a return to madrasa teaching. Since the scholar was compelled to cooperate, he is freed of responsibility.

As was the case with most rural notables, the tenor of Mansuri relations with French authorities changed significantly over time. Through the 1930s, relations remained correct and reasonably cordial. Reports of Qadi Ahmad's activities in the "heroic" early days of the protectorate were faithfully passed along to new administrators in his confidential intelligence dossier.[1] As is standard in such reports, his politically important family ties are listed as are his properties, although as mentioned in Chapter Five, the size of his agricultural holdings and herds are underreported by roughly half: four houses, fourteen gardens, two hundred hectares of cultivated land, two mules, fourteen cows and four hundred sheep. The report continues that Qadi Ahmad is distinguished (*ittalāʿ*) in his knowledge of Islamic scholarship and possesses a "first class diploma" [sic] from the Yusufiya. "He knows Arabic literature and is informed on modern social life. He is considered to be a just qadi and is respected, enjoying a major influence in the entire region. He is helpful toward the French and has the aptitude to be appointed a qadi in a city or a qaid in a rural area."

THE WAR YEARS

Protectorate rural administration worked reasonably well until the Second World War. Many civil and military administrators were rapidly trained to replace officers who refused to

---

[1] A copy of this document was taken from official files in Casablanca, translated into Arabic by Saʿid Guessous, a translator-interpreter working with the French administration, and mailed to Qadi Ahmad. Evidently the mails were often regarded as secure. I saw the document preserved in its original envelope. The report was written by Captain "Dulur" [the name is given only in Arabic transcription], Chief of the Bureau des Affaires Indigènes of Ntifa and Azilal, and is dated June 25, 1937.

serve with Vichy or who had earlier chosen to return to France for active military service.[2] More important than the declining quality of available administrators were the economic and political dislocations of the war years and a renewed impetus to the nationalist movement from the realization that the French were not invincible.

In the course of our discussions, 'Abd ar-Rahman was the first to raise the subject of the declining quality of French administrators in the war years. He observed that the French began to recruit their officers from a different category of persons in France. My notes on August 28, 1969 record:

> He asked me whether there wasn't an equivalent to shurfa in France, who all had pierced ears so that they could recognize one another. I asked him whether he ever saw an A.I. officer or civil controller with a pierced ear. 'Abd ar-Rahman replied that he had not, but only "heard" that French shurfa had distinguishing marks. I tried to explain as best as I could the hidden marks of social class in France—language, style, and attitudes toward society.

'Abd ar-Rahman's concept of divisions in French society, like his perceptions of the European war, "the fuss in Europe" (aṣ-ṣdāʿ fī-ʿurūba) is imperfect. European society is at the periphery of his social imagination, and is as blurred as counterpart French colonial visions of the Moroccan social order. In contrast, his comments on French local policy during the war years are concrete and precise. 'Abd ar-Rahman says that the "non-shurfa" administrators of these years had orders to follow the lead of local qaids, who were assumed to know how to "handle" the populations under their jurisdiction. After the defeat of France by the Germans, colonial officials

---

[2] For an excellent general account of the rise and fall of the French native affairs administration in rural Morocco, see Bidwell (1973). Vincent Monteil (1961), himself a onetime Affaires Indigènes officer, provides a thoughtful complementary "insider's" account.

were also concerned that an uprising against colonial rule might occur in Morocco.[3]

Whatever the deficiencies of personnel assigned to rural posts in Morocco during the Vichy years, the officer in charge of the Azilal post for seven years beginning in 1941 achieved the grudging respect of the Mansuri brothers. A surviving fragment of 'Abd ar-Rahman's diary, written on March 4, 1948, the day that Captain Fist left Azilal, describes the hakim as a "human devil" (*insān min ash-shayāṭīn*), the only instance in which such extraordinary language occurs in his writing.[4] According to the diary entry, Captain Fist was a fencer and skilled horseman, married to an "American." This is an extraordinarily remote possibility for a French colonial officer of the period. Given the presence of Americans in Morocco after the Allied landings, 'Abd ar-Rahman appears to have assumed that all non-French foreigners of the period were American. Fist was so fluent in classical Arabic that he could speak for half an hour without error or pause.

Although recognizing his extraordinary qualities, the diary also describes Fist as perfidious (*fīh al-khdāʿ*). He introduced a network of spies and informers into the region, held back the distribution of some ration coupons to sell them on the black market and, despite the presence of his "American" wife, cavorted with dancer/prostitutes (*shaykhāt*). The quasi-heroic and contradictory qualities attributed to Fist indicate how peripheral the European presence was to the society and administration as experienced by 'Abd ar-Rahman, despite the fact of colonial political and economic domination.

[3] In July 1941, a secret circular from the office of the Resident-General ordered each local post to draw up contingency plans for the defense of French administrators and settlers in rural areas. Cabinet du Résident-Général, circular 422 DM, dated July 4, 1941. Copy preserved in the file, "Securité locale," archives of the Contrôle Civil, Boujad.

[4] I have been unsuccessful in efforts to identify this officer more precisely. In any case, what is important in the present context is 'Abd ar-Rahman's conception of the officer. 'Abd ar-Rahman thinks that he was transferred to a post near Fez, and that he died in the early 1950s.

It would have been difficult for any Native Affairs officer to have been liked by tribesmen or notables as political and economic conditions progressively deteriorated. The use of corvée labor was intensified. To feed France and Morocco's urban population, Vichy introduced food rationing, even to rural regions, and requisitioned crops and livestock against paper money that was almost worthless because there was nothing to buy with it. The black market flourished, often with the connivance of local officials. Whatever the alleged deficiencies of Fist's character, 'Abd ar-Rahman grudgingly admitted that the captain knew with precision what occurred in his jurisdiction and extracted the maximum resources from it.

The Mansuri brothers had had reasonably good relations with earlier local officials. With Fist, there was animosity from the beginning. Once the captain's coolness toward the Mansuris became public knowledge, those engaged in land disputes and other quarrels with them initiated denunciations, often anonymous, against them, knowing that they had a receptive audience. Cordial relations with earlier officers had insulated the Mansuris from such attacks.

An initial cause of contention between Fist and the Mansuri brothers was a late-model Dodge that Qadi Ahmad imported just before wartime restrictions were imposed. At the time, only the sultan possessed the same model of automobile in Morocco. Because of fuel rationing, Qadi Ahmad put the Dodge up on blocks and used another, smaller vehicle that consumed less fuel. Later, when the sultan required a spare part for his own vehicle, he sent his chauffeur to Bzu for it. Qadi Ahmad willingly stripped it from his car. Fist was furious. He wanted the Dodge for himself. Fist cut off the food rationing coupons of the two brothers. A Jewish merchant in a nearby town managed clandestinely to deliver food to them in the night.

Qadi Ahmad responded in kind. He wrote an anonymous letter denouncing Fist to his superiors. Because of restrictions on travel and the risk of immediate detection if the letter were mailed locally, Qadi Ahmad gave the letter to a Bzu merchant with a travel permit, who posted it in Casablanca. Fist suspected the Mansuri brothers of orchestrating local protests against his conduct, an act that he regarded as sedition (*fitna*).

One reason for his suspicions were the brothers' informal communications with the palace. Especially after his meeting in Anfa, near Casablanca, with Roosevelt and Churchill on January 22, 1943 (Hassan II 1978: 29-30), the monarch disregarded official channels for communicating with local officials and contacted them directly. On January 11 of the following year, the leaders of Morocco's Istiqlal (Independence) party gave the monarch a copy of their manifesto, which included the demand for independence. Under intense French pressure, Sidi Muhammad bin Yusif issued a statement that the word "independence" should not be used. The Istiqlal party, which until that year had received its support primarily from the urban bourgeoisie, began to achieve a much wider base of popular support. Recognizing this, the French initiated a wave of arrests in February 1944, which included a number of prominent men of learning (Julien 1972: 198-199). Despite French intimidation, the ruler maintained informal channels of communication. An unsigned note on fine paper dated October 31, 1945, summoned Qadi Ahmad to the sultan in Rabat, just as the sultan summoned scores of other local notables to take measure of his support. It also said that the king "was pleased with his actions and aware of what Hajj Ahmad was doing," a sentiment ambiguous enough to withstand possible French interception. The Qadi traveled to Rabat without formal permission from the French, thus earning more censure from local authorities.

In 1944 there were violent pronationalist riots in the major cities. The French suspected collusion between the Palace and nationalist leaders, and there was a wave of repression in which both nationalist leaders and men of learning were interrogated and imprisoned (Bernard 1968: 24). The accusation of suspected nationalist activity, like the legal offense of having a *mauvais esprit*, was increasingly used as a tool of intimidation by colonial authorities, who now had added pretexts to intervene in local quarrels. Fist received letters denouncing the Mansuri brothers for giving money to 'Allal al-Fassi and the Istiqlal movement. 'Abd ar-Rahman says that they never made such contributions, but his brother's contacts with the palace and refusal to denounce local nationalists led them both to be suspect. By late 1944, open hostilities between Fist and the Mansuris were attenuated by a personal visit from Hajj Thami al-Glawi to Bzu, said to be acting on instructions from the monarch. Hajj Thami arranged a reconciliation between Fist and the Mansuri brothers, and brought an end to several other outstanding disputes in the region.

'Abd ar-Rahman's surviving notebooks for the 1944-1946 period contain a mixture of information on local events and radio news: the end of the Second World War in Europe (May 8, 1945), the resignation of De Gaulle (January 21, 1946), and commemorative verses written by men of learning. The most striking element of the diary is its relentless recording of local economic conditions. It is difficult to provide meaningful conversion figures for the rapid fluctuations in currency in the last days of Vichy, but the dramatic escalation of prices as commodities disappeared from the market indicates the increasing gravity of the situation.

A prolonged drought and famine in 1945-1946 exacerbated conditions. 'Abd ar-Rahman's penciled diary entries record the lack of rain, massive crop failures, and the widespread death of animals and humans from starvation and typhus. In the immediate vicinity of Bzu, he records that 5,000 persons died between 1941 and 1944 (1360-1363). When finally rains fell for a week in 1944, they were immediately followed by an attack of locusts that stripped even the bark from trees. Despite these hardships, the French intensified the corvée and requisitioned the meager crops of olives and oranges. In famine conditions, law and order broke down. Tribesmen took to killing travelers, and no one was brought to justice. By

TABLE 4. PRICE INCREASES IN BZU, 1942–1944

Commodity	Unit of Measure	1942	1944	Inflation Rate (%)
Barley	'abra*	10 F.	1,000 F.	10,000
Wheat	'abra	200	1,500	750
Mutton	kilo	10	150	1,500
Chickens	each	15	225	1,500
Sugar	kilo	7	2,000	28,571
Tea	kilo	30	400	1,333
Olives	kilo	10	250	2,500
Lard	kilo	15	250	1,667
Honey	kilo	20	250	1,250
Candles	each	3	100†	3,333
Charcoal	kilo	2	100†	2,500
Cotton fabric:				
men's clothing	meter	2	3,500	175,000
women's		6	†	
"Heavy"				
textiles	meter	10	800	8,000
Silk				
(black market)	meter	10	7,500	7,500
Sargha (cloth				
for jallabas)	meter	150	5,000†	3,333
Iron	kilo	2	50	2,500
Balgha				
(trad. shoes):				
Men's	pair	30	750	2,500
Women's		40	2,500	6,250

* Lit. "measure." A local measure used for cereals; equivalent to 12 kilograms in Bzu.
† Subsequently disappeared from the market.
SOURCE: Diary of Hajj 'Abd ar-Rahman, 1944.

early 1946 in the Ntifa region, 11,000 deaths were attributed to typhus. Pestilence took over from hunger and cold as the leading cause of death. Some wealthy merchants and notables made enormous profits from the black market during this period. Others, especially during the 1945 famine, massively expanded their landholdings by purchasing land and houses for a few measures of grain, turning tribesmen into share-croppers and townsmen into tenants.

Conditions improved after September 1945, when food and seeds provided by American aid began to be distributed through the colonial administration. 'Abd ar-Rahman wrote in his diary in that month, "Because of the great dollar, people were freed from famime. People thanked God for what the Americans did and recognized the greatness and goodness of the American empire" (*dawla*). He also wrote a qasida in praise of the occasion. The price of wheat fell from 1,500 francs to 750 francs, and that of barley from 1,000 francs to 45 francs.

The Fist era came to an end precisely on March 4, 1948. On that date he summoned the notables of the region to Azilal—shaykhs, qadis, and qaids—and ordered the qaids to bring tribesmen on horseback. French officers from other regions were also present. Fist reviewed the assembly, shook the hand of each in farewell, and then provided a lunch for the notables. 'Abd ar-Rahman's diary records that the real celebrations began once he left the region.

Postwar Nationalism

For a brief period after the Second World War, especially during the tenure of Eirik Labonne as Resident-General (1946-1947), colonial policy became liberal and reformist. Agricultural development schemes were initiated and major efforts were made to expand facilities for health and education. Pressure from colons and the more conservative elements of the colonial administration soon eviscerated the most basic reforms, especially efforts to modernize indigenous agricultural production (see Berque and Couleau 1946; Bidwell 1973:228-232).

A key political event reflecting changed Moroccan sensibilities toward colonial rule was a speech delivered by Sidi Muhammad bin Yusif in Tangier on April 10, 1947, the text of which had been submitted under pressure to the French for prior approval. Three days before the king's speech, Senegalese troops in Casablanca opened fire on demonstrators, leaving hundreds of casualties. When the king delivered his speech in Tangier, he left out a phrase praising the French (Julien 1972: 311). Moroccan nationalists enthusiastically welcomed this first public indication of the king's opposition to the French. On May 14, 1947, Labonne was replaced as a consequence of this incident by General Alphonse Juin, who sought through vigorous police action to suppress the nationalists and to compel the Palace to disown them. Under intense pressure, the monarch agreed to restate his loyalty to France, but refused to speak against the nationalist movement. Repression intensified and Juin became increasingly impatient with the silence of the palace (Julien 1972: 324-326).

The main consequence for Bzu of the brief postwar liberal interlude were plans to expand the French administrative presence, which, however, were implemented only after the return to more repressive colonial policies. In June 1949 a Captain "Boeuf" arrived in Bzu. In addition to overseeing construction of the new administrative center and adjacent houses for government employees, he supervised construction of a bridge for one of the major access roads to the Bzu market and set up Bzu's first electric generator. It provided electricity for the administrative center, a school, and a few nearby houses for civil servants. Boeuf amazed villagers by performing manual labor alongside his workers, and paid wages rather than relying upon the detested earlier practice of the corvée.

The administrative center was officially opened on December 12, 1949. A feast marked the occasion, attended by the Moroccan notables of the region and key regional French officials: "Talig" (Bni Millal), "Alexandre" and "Gamsi" (Azilal) and "Doyen" (Tanant). The qaid of Azilal had until then successfully opposed the opening of additional French administrative centers, correctly sensing that an expansion of the French administration would diminish his own influence.

Prior to 1949, the French Native Affairs officer was present in Bzu only the weekly market day.

The strongest indication of a shift in popular sentiment toward the monarchy during the 1940s was the widespread replacement of the title "sultan" with the more "modern" usage of "king" (mālik), a usage that first gained currency among the educated in the 1930s. For the French, the ruler of Morocco was the sultan, and his entity of rule was the Sharifian Empire, concepts that nationalists regarded as archaic. "King," in contrast, delineated the ruler of a specifically delimited territory. For the French, use of the title "king" was evidence of nationalist agitation and therefore illegal.

Although the French sought to discourage travel by the monarch in the late 1940s, they allowed the leaders of complaisant religious orders to circulate freely, collecting gifts and donations from their remaining supporters. 'Abd al-Hayy al-Kittani continued to travel throughout Morocco with the blessings of the French, as did Ḥājj 'Abd as-Salām an-Nāṣirī, head of the the Nasiri religious order in Tamgrut. Hajj 'Abd as-Salam last visited Bzu in a car surrounded by fifty splendidly dressed, armed retainers on horseback in 1949. 'Abd ar-Rahman described his "progress" (ḥarka) as being "like that of the sultan." Such visits nonetheless ceased after 1949, as the safety of these religious leaders in their travels could no longer be assured because of their open support for the French.

When the king was allowed to travel, he was enthusiastically received. In April 1950 he visited Marrakesh. 'Abd ar-Rahman's diary records the visit. To get a glimpse of their ruler, crowds, including 'Abd ar-Rahman, lined his intended route from early in the morning. At 10:20, Sidi Muhammad bin Yusif got out of his automobile in Jama'a al-Fna', entered the madina and walked to the Yusufiya. Carpets were spread over the entire route. Although the walk was a short one and the monarch was not permitted by the French to make a speech or to pause at the Yusufiya, he returned to the motorcade only at 11:15. Along the route, spectators continuously chanted "Long Live the King!" and "Long Live the 'Alawi dynasty!," words that ordinarily led to arrest. 'Abd ar-Rah-man recorded: "Those lining the route cried out these slogans until the colonialists (al-mustaʿmirīn) wanted to close their ears." The king then proceeded to the pasha's house in Ryāḍ Zaytūn for lunch, and in the evening met there with the men of learning of the Yusufiya.

As with any royal progress, there was competition among local notables to entertain the king and his entourage. One spinoff of the monarch's visit was a separate visit to Bzu by several ranking members of his entourage, including Madanī bin al-Ḥuṣnī of the Ministry of Justice, the historian Muḥam-mad bin 'Abbās al-Kabbāj, the ubiquitous poet Hasan al-Bu Naʿmani, and Mukhtar as-Susi. The member of the group who arranged the visit, Ḥasan bin Aḥmad bin Masʿūd, was a close friend of Qadi Ahmad. He sent a letter in advance (dated April 23) from Marrakesh announcing their arrival time and specified the desired menu. For one dish he even provided the recipe, just in case the preparation of the Rabati speciality was unknown in rustic Bzu. The visit, of course, reaffirmed the prominence of the Mansuris.

The Mansuris were so firmly entrenched in the administra-tive apparatus of rural Morocco that they could occasionally get their way over the objections of local French authorities. In September 1950, local French authorities at first denied 'Abd ar-Rahman permission to go on the pilgrimage, a key event for which he had been planning for years. For the French, participation in the pilgrimage was a potential danger. It usually entailed visits en route to Arab countries antago-nistic to colonial rule. Withholding permission was also a stick to be used against lukewarm local officials. For 'Abd ar-Rah-man, it was interference with one of his most important ob-ligations as a Muslim. In undertaking the pilgrimage, a Mus-lim undertakes formally to commit the rest of his life to God. Almost the only decorations in 'Abd ar-Rahman's house, in addition to portraits of Morocco's present king and Sidi Mu-hammad bin Yusif, is one of 'Abd ar-Rahman himself, taken upon his return from Mekka, together with the prayer-mat he used there and other souvenirs. The pilgrimage had profound meaning to him.

To secure permission to undertake it, he used the complex lines of communication available to established notables to bypass the local French hierarchy. The contact that eventually worked was established through an influential notary in Marrakesh of Bzu origin, who maintained amicable relations with the French and the Glawi, although he had clandestinely cast his lot with the king and the Istiqlal party.[5] Another channel was through his wife's family, distant relations of Hajj Thami al-Glawi. Finally the pasha's son, Ibrahim al-Glawi, wrote a letter on 'Abd ar-Rahman's behalf to Philippe Boniface, commandant of the Casablanca region, who authorized 'Abd ar-Rahman to leave for the pilgrimage in September. By that time, however, 'Abd ar-Rahman decided not to go. Participation in the pilgrimage in 1950 would have been construed by most Moroccans as a sign of collaboration with the French. Only after Independence, in 1960, did he actually leave for Mecca, returning by way of Spain in order to visit the former Islamic capitals of Granada and Cordoba. This was the only occasion on which he ever left Morocco.

The Mansuri brothers, like most other men of learning, followed the cautious political lead of Sidi Muhammad bin Yusif. The monarch carefully avoided direct confrontation with French authorities, but at the same time lent tacit support to nationalist leaders. Relations with the French and their Moroccan allies became increasingly bitter. Finally, there was a face-to-face confrontation between Hajj Thami al-Glawi and the king, in which the pasha of Marrakesh informed the monarch that he was the sultan of the Istiqlal party and not of Morocco (Julien 1972: 324). When the encounter was first publicly reported, Mukhtar as-Susi was a guest of the Mansuris in Bzu.

[5] Interview, Mūlāy Ḥasan al-Bzīwī, Marrakesh, July 26, 1976. From 1949 to 1952, Mulay Hasan was deputy pasha of Marrakesh. His role as a confidential informant for the king went undetected until 1952, when the pasha succeeded in removing him from office.

When [Mukhtar as-Susi] first heard the news on the radio, he said nothing. Later in the day, he asked Qadi Ahmad to accompany him on a long walk. He told the qadi that he would have to leave the next day. My brother protested that he had just arrived, but he insisted he must leave to put his affairs in order. Indeed, soon afterward he was arrested by the French.

THE DEPOSITION

To justify their increasing pressure against the king, the French encouraged Hajj Thami al-Glawi to circulate a petition denouncing Sidi Muhammad bin Yusif for, among other matters, his disregard of Islamic values. 'Abd ar-Rahman claimed that even Hajj Thami al-Glawi was against the wording of the petition and "raised his hand" against it, although in the end he yielded to the French. When the petition was circulated, notables were told that it was against communism. Most would not have signed if they knew its actual content. The qaids of the southern regions of Morocco, for the most part poorly educated or illiterate, readily signed. Most men of learning, including the Mansuri brothers, refused to do so despite intimidation and threats.

The French deposed the monarch on August 20, 1953, exiling him and his immediate family to Madagascar. He was replaced by a reluctant and ineffectual distant relative, Muhammad bin 'Arafa. It became increasingly difficult to remain uncommitted in the struggle against the French. After the monarch's deposition, ostensibly carried out at the request of Moroccan notables, men of learning were expected to offer an oath of fealty (bay'a) to the "puppet" sultan. Most refused to do so. The attitude of most was that withholding consent was in itself a sufficient political statement. Both the French and their Moroccan supporters such as Hajj Thami al-Glawi freely used threats and intimidation to secure compliance to their will.

The day after the exile of Sidi Muhammad bin Yusif was

the Feast of Abraham ('Id al-Kabir) in Morocco, a day on which the entire community of men assemble for collective prayers at the prayer-ground (*mṣalla*) adjoining every Moroccan town. As a prelude to the sermon delivered on such occasions, each prayer-leader customarily recites an oath of fealty to the reigning sultan. At the time, 'Abd ar-Rahman was imam for Bzu.

> That day, when I went to the prayer-ground to say the sermon, I left the keys to the house with my wife. I had never done that before. I said to her: "I don't know what will happen. I don't know if I will return. Take the keys and look after the children. When I got to the msalla, I saw members of the Foreign Legion on a ridge overlooking the assembly, with machine guns trained on us. By the time the sermon was over, everyone was in tears.

I asked 'Abd ar-Rahman in whose name he said the sermon.

> I got to "in the name of the sultan," then I coughed. I didn't pronounce the sermon in the name of any sultan.

But you could have, I persisted.

> Yes, but to have said it in the name of Muhammad bin Yusif would have been sedition to the French. To have said it in the name of Muhammad bin 'Arafa would have been a lie. It would have been against the shra'. So I said nothing clearly. And everyone went away weeping. The French were very afraid that night. Before morning, sixteen people were arrested in Bzu.

A declaration in the name of the deposed sultan would have been a futile gesture, and therefore an "unreasonable" one. French troops were present and there was no way in which the immediate return of the deposed king could have been realized. Nonetheless, 'Abd ar-Rahman was unwilling to compromise his Islamic principles and declare an oath of fealty to an illegitimate ruler.

The Mansuri brothers did nothing to affirm the legitimacy

of Muhammad bin 'Arafa, but neither did they overtly work for his fall. In a term of self-description current among many men of learning of the period, they were *neutre*, a term that entered colloquial Moroccan Arabic after 1953 and that carried a very special contextual meaning. As in prior times of political crisis in Morocco (Burke 1972; 1976), men of learning were reluctant to enter the political arena, but being "neutral" was in itself a political act that increasingly paralyzed the French administrative apparatus. They remained overtly aloof from the nationalists, but withheld support from the French. They knew who the local nationalists were and who participated in the terrorist bands that became increasingly active after the monarch's exile. Support for Muhammad bin Yusif indirectly united nationalists and "neutrals."

To the French, Moroccans could assert that their neutrality implied nothing more than political noninvolvement, precisely the sort of attitude colonial officials encouraged all along. Virtually all work in the Islamic law courts and the "traditional" law courts in Berber regions ceased. Court officials declined to recognize the legitimacy of the ruler in whose name they were expected to act. They appeared at their places of employment, but performed no work.

In their own way, men of learning were just as effective in paralyzing the work of the protectorate as were nationalist merchants in paralyzing food distribution systems and militant dockworkers in controlling the Casablanca port. An open declaration in support of the exiled sultan brought swift punishment and immediate removal from office. Being "neutral" tied up the French in their own style of feint and required time-consuming actions against individual officials. Moreover, the information the French needed to proceed against individuals ultimately had to come from Moroccans themselves. Even the pasha of Marrakesh, to whom the French provided an unrestrained hand in suppressing opponents to their policies, were held back from decisive action by the complex, interlocking ties among notables. No one was certain of the outcome of events, so that most Moroccans temporized rather than openly take sides. At the same time, the rhythm of strikes, sabotage, and open violence dramatically increased (Le Tourneau 1962: 233, 238-244).

As in earlier periods under French colonial rule, ties of kinship and friendship with officials elsewhere in Morocco kept the Mansuri brothers informed of hostile moves against them. By 1954 the French began to remove from office Moroccans suspected of supporting the deposed monarch. Many officials and notables were imprisoned and had their lands and other property confiscated. The local administrator in Bzu recommended prison for Qadi Ahmad and the confiscation of his properties. The recommendation was vetoed by his immediate superior in Azilal, Alexandre, an officer with decades of experience in the region. Alexandre appeared to be aware that the decision to depose the king had been maladroit and numbered the days of colonial Morocco. 'Abd ar-Rahman narrated:

> Alexandre summoned the qadi to Azilal. There he asked him whether it was true that he said to Hajj Thami al-Glawi that he still recognized only Muhammad bin Yusif as sultan. The qadi replied that he was a "friend of France" (a conventional phrase often used by the deposed monarch himself) but that the only sultan he recognized was Muhammad bin Yusif. Another French officer, also present, suggested that the only hope of the qadi to avoid exile and confiscation of his lands was to seek the pardon of 'Abd al-Hayy al-Kittani.

> Alexandre then asked the qadi to step outside, in order to speak with him in private. He proposed that the qadi accept a transfer to as-Swira for a few years. In time, he said, death by old age would overtake Muhammad bin 'Arafa and Hajj Thami, and by then Muhammad bin Yusif might well return to the throne. Alexandre also told my brother that the Glawi was rapidly losing his ability

to influence events. My brother listened to Alexandre and left for as-Swira.

"Why did Alexandre do this for your brother?"

Alexandre understood the situation like a French noble. He had worked earlier with Qadi Ahmad and spoke excellent Arabic. He argued with his superiors that if the Mansuris or their properties were touched because of the incident in the msalla or their refusal to recognize Muhammad bin 'Arafa, it would be like lighting a fire under the earth that would build up and eventually lead to an explosion. Alexandre knew the reputation of our father, of how tribesmen paid the first taxes thinking they were alms. He feared an uprising.

So a French officer invoked his reading of local tradition with his superiors to head off a local confrontation with erstwhile Moroccan colleagues. In January 1954 Qadi Ahmad left for as-Swira, but by April was removed from his official functions there for unspecified "administrative reasons." Nonetheless, he remained in as-Swira for two years and three months, until Morocco's independence in March 1956. For the first time since becoming his brother's deputy in 1932, 'Abd ar-Rahman officially assumed the function of qadi in Bzu in January 1954, although he too was removed from his post in April. In November 1955, when Sidi Muhammad bin Yusif returned from exile, the two brothers sought an audience with him in Rabat. Qadi Ahmad was so overcome with emotion that he cried in their monarch's presence, leaving his younger brother to speak for the two. 'Abd ar-Rahman simply declared that the two of them were following the path set for them by their monarch (*Sidna*), and the king thanked them. The audience lasted five minutes.

INDEPENDENCE: THE VIEW FROM THE PERIPHERY

Many Moroccans enthusiastically anticipated the beginning of a new social and economic order in 1956. Yet by the 1970s, a leading Moroccan intellectual could write in retrospect that the post-1956 Moroccan government was not a "resumption of the precolonial past, but a continuation of the regime of the Protectorate" (Laroui 1974: 53; 1977a: 348). In the first few years after independence, it appeared as if rural notables, for the most part compromised with the protectorate, were to be shunted aside in favor of the urban bourgeosie, who formed the backbone of nationalist leadership, provided the cadres of the new administration, and supported most of the new government's plans for industrialization and modernization, much of which were inherited from the last years of French rule. In 1958 a decree was passed that sequestered the property of "feudal and traiterous elements," principally the rural elite, although it was never vigorously applied (Leveau 1977: 275).

In retrospect it is possible to discern, as does Laroui, a strong continuity between the protectorate and postcolonial regimes. For persons who lived through the often violent events of this period, no such continuity was apparent at the time. Yet almost without exception, the families of notables influential under the protectorate remained in place after independence. In the turbulent first years after independence, the monarchy came to realize that one of its principal pillars was the category of landed rural notables, who also constituted the bulwark of the former protectorate (Marais 1969; Leveau 1977). After a period of indecision, by 1960 the monarchy decided to avoid measures that would alienate the support of rural notables (Leveau 1977: 273-278; Marais 1969; Gellner 1973).

On the one hand, the Mansuri brothers were denounced by their enemies during the protectorate as nationalist supporters, and their refusal to acquiesce in the deposition of Muhammad bin Yusif cost them their sinecures in the judiciary and threatened the confiscation of their lands. On the other hand, after independence, the nationalists accused them of collaboration. Such accusations caused temporary setbacks for rural notables in many regions of Morocco, but Qadi Ahmad's ties with the Palace, and probably his reputation with liberal French administrators who remained at their posts to ease the transition to independence, insulated him from the excesses to which other rural notables were sometimes exposed.

The months before and after independence in March 1956 were a confused period. Immediately after independence, Qadi Ahmad was appointed simultaneously in two separate decrees as qaid and qadi of Ntifa, although after a month and seven days the qadiship was taken away from him, leaving him to continue reluctantly in his role as qaid. Because the judiciary in rural Morocco was in general not seriously compromised by their prior dealings with the French, many qadis found themselves the only available persons to work with the new Ministry of the Interior in rural areas.[6] Ahmad Mansuri submitted his resignation on February 28, 1957. It was finally accepted on June 17. As a sign of the continued esteem in which he was held by Muhammad bin Yusif, he was appointed to Morocco's Constitutional Council in 1960. Indicative of his local support, he was subsequently elected a delegate to Morocco's first parliament in 1963, the last formal function he was to exercise prior to his death on March 6, 1975.

Qadi Ahmad's appointment as qaid was made over the opposition of local activists in the Istiqlal party. In the first years after independence, the monarchy was still uncertain of its strength and, as 'Abd ar-Rahman recalled, local leaders of the Istiqlal party installed themselves as necessary intermediaries to the administration. Urban militants of the party were frequently made administrators of rural areas, but their inexperience and unfamiliarity with the rural milieu handicapped effective administration. Prior to independence, a modest monthly subscription had bought membership in the Istiqlal party, but after independence, the cost of adhesion

---

[6] Interview, Hajj Aḥmad bin 'Abd as-Salām al-Bū 'Ayyāshī, Tangier, June 23, 1973. Hajj Ahmad, himself a qadi in Spanish Morocco, found himself appointed as a "super-qaid" (qā'id mumtāz) shortly after independence, although like others in his situation, he spent his efforts in securing a transfer back to the Ministry of Justice.

escalated considerably as persons who had stood on the sidelines sought to insure their future. Every application to the government for employment, use of forest lands, adjustment of taxes, went forward only with a recommendation by the local Istiqlal bureau.

As for 'Abd ar-Rahman, his first appointment came nearly a year later. In independent Morocco, the greatest urgency was attached to insuring continuity in the Ministry of the Interior. Local appointments to the judiciary took somewhat longer. On May 6, 1957, while he was overseeing the use of a mechanical harvester on his fields, he was brought a message to return to Bzu immediately for a telephone call from the minister of justice, 'Abd al-Krīm bin Jallūn, offering him the post of qadi of Boujad. He accepted. The official proclamation arrived nine days later.

For 'Abd ar-Rahman's generation, there is a close link between the structure and goals of religious orders and those of political parties (hizb) (cf. Rezette 1955: 27), an attitude not dispelled by his experiences of political interference with the Islamic judiciary in the first years of independence. "They fight with one another and deceive people to win their support. Like the brotherhoods, the political parties are primarily interested in pulling political power in their direction (ta-yjurru l-quwwāt)." As a key example, he cited the practice of the Istiqlal party in the early 1950s of requiring adherents to swear an oath (qasm) on the Quran, a practice also used by some brotherhoods and taken very seriously. 'Abd ar-Rahman considers such oaths to be bid'a. Many early nationalist meetings were also held in mosques. Men now in their forties and fifties continue to vote for the Istiqlal party in Morocco, even though it is rapidly declining in popular support, because of the oath they swore years earlier.

When 'Abd ar-Rahman arrived in Boujad as judge in 1957, the Istiqlal party was still more important than the local administration. It successfully "sponsored" all routine administrative requests and sought to intervene in the Islamic

court, a move that 'Abd ar-Rahman says he successfully opposed. The fragmentation of the Istiqlal party into various
factions (ta'ifas) shortly after independence is interpreted by
'Abd ar-Rahman as just another sign of the concern of political
leaders with nothing but opportunities for themselves.

A second element to contend with in rural areas immediately
after independence, especially in southern Morocco, was the
self-proclaimed units of the Army of Liberation (jaysh at-
taḥrīr). In some regions efforts were made to incorporate these
bands into the newly formed Moroccan army. Elsewhere the
activities of independent units increased rather than dimin-
ished with independence, suggesting a hazy demarcation between brigandage and politically motivated terrorism. For
'Abd ar-Rahman, participants in the Liberation Army were
prone to anarchy (sība) because they failed to ascertain the
wishes of the monarch, the source of legitimate Islamic authority. By failing to do so, they were in his judgment no
better than the rioters in Marrakesh in 1956 who burned to
death several of the Glawi's most notorious collaborators (see
Maxwell 1966: 266-268).

Liberation Army units were active in Bzu, especially after
France announced its intention to grant independence to Morocco. 'Abd ar-Rahman describes one incident:

> A squad of them came to me one day [after independence]
> in Bzu. They were from the region, but not from Bzu
> itself. They all had rifles. I didn't know them, but they
> knew my brother and myself. My brother was qaid in
> Azilal at the time. They knew his reputation as a tough
> man, so they spoke to me instead. They said they wanted
> our car, so that they could go on a mission to "visit" a
> traitor [name deleted], who was a qaid in the Protecto-
> rate. All those who worked for the Protectorate were
> being threatened.

"Who gave you the orders to kill him?" I asked. "Was it the
sultan?"

They replied that they didn't know the sultan. All they knew was 'Allal [al-Fassi] and the [Istiqlal] party. Often they chose their own targets. They took our car and went that night to the qaid's, but he put up a fight, killed one of them, and escaped. They killed the qaid's son, though. For that they got five years in prison.

At first, the sultan said nothing. He watched these things happen. Once he knew where his power was, he began moving against [the Liberation Army]. They had become like the [political] parties, always looking for money. Later the sultan also moved to limit the power of the parties. People were becoming afraid of the Istiqlal party because if the Istiqlal said that someone was against them, the man might be dead not long after.

The idea that at least some political leaders might have been motivated by notions of social justice was difficult for 'Abd ar-Rahman to comprehend. For him and like-minded men of learning, men's responsibilities toward one another were those laid out in the Quran and in Islamic law. As understood by Hajj 'Abd ar-Rahman, these responsibilities delineate individual ethics and ignore the presence of classes and social groups (cf. Kessler 1978: 210-213). 'Abd ar-Rahman's concern is principally with how to guide individual conduct by the higher principles of the word of God as known through the Quran, the traditions of the Prophet, and Islamic law. Such concepts explicitly restrain and control base self-interest, but do not easily lead to collective notions of social justice.

SEVEN

The Great Transformation?

THE EROSION OF TRADITIONAL LEARNING

'Abd ar-Rahman became qadi in a world substantially different from that for which he had been educated. By 1957, higher
religious learning was an empty shell of its former self. Men
of learning retained widespread popular respect but their numbers were no longer being reproduced. Yet men of learning
voiced no sense of crisis. No major efforts were made to
sustain religious education in its older form.

When alternatives to the mosque-university developed on
a wide scale in the 1930s, higher Islamic education quickly
lost its former vitality. Its sudden decline can be attributed to
a relatively straightforward conjunction of events. First was
the French "organization" of Morocco's two principal
mosque-universities, the Qarawiyin in 1931 and the Yusufiya
in 1939, undertaken ostensibly to improve the standard of
learning. These "reforms" came in the wake of major protests
against French rule in which the mosque-universities had
played a role (al-Fassi 1954: 128-129, 133-135). French "organization" made the faculty salaried civil servants subject to
governmental control. Those teachers remaining in the organized institutions suffered a significant loss of popular prestige. Gifts to them by pious Moroccans, rich and poor, virtually ceased. Rather than teach in the "organized" milieu of
the Qarawiyin after 1931, several of its leading teachers left
for elsewhere in the country, including the Yusufiya and
mosques in smaller towns. A similar exodus occurred from
the Yusufiya when organization was imposed upon it in November 1939.

The procedure used by the French to appoint mosque-university leadership was identical to that used for the appointment of local officials. Protectorate authorities proposed three candidates to the sultan, leaving him the final choice. In the shell game of the protectorate, the French still reserved the right to veto the sultan's selection.[1] The Yusufiya was given a rector and a Scholarly Council (al-Majlis al-'Ilmī), composed of leading teachers at the Yusufiya.

The work of the rector and the Scholarly Council was monitored by a controller (murāqib) empowered to veto decisions reached by the scholarly council. The appointment of controller did not require the sultan's approval and thus served as a useful check upon possible actions by the Council. From the "organization" of the Yusufiya until August 1953, the controller was Muhammad Būrghba, known to have been working for French intelligence. After Muhammad bin Yusif's deposition, he was appointed Minister of Pious Endowments under the "puppet" sultan, Bu 'Arafa. Burghba was subsequently killed during the April 1956 riots, a month after independence, in Marrakesh (Maxwell 1966: 266-268). Burghba's replacement as controller for the last two years of colonial rule was 'Abd al-Wahhāb aṣ-Ṣahrāwī ad-Dukkālī.

The four successive rectors under French rule were respected scholars. The first was Mulay Mubārik al-Amrānī, originally a learned shaykh of a religious lodge in Tafilalt, in southern Morocco. In January 1941 al-Amrani left for the Qarawiyin and was replaced by Muhammad ibn 'Uthmān, a reformist who had studied for eight years at the al-Azhar in Cairo and wrote a book on the Yusufiya's early history ('Uthmān 1935). Former students remember him with affection because he dis-

---

[1] This discussion is based upon events at the Yusufiya, although procedures at the Qarawiyin appear to have been broadly analogous. I am especially indebted to at-Touarti 'Alī bin al-Mu'allim, a former member of the Yusufiyya's Scholarly Council, ardent bibliophile, confidant of Mukhtar as-Susi and, in the late 1950s, liquidator of the estate of Hajj Thami al-Glawi, for sharing with me his perceptive comments on the workings of the Yusufiya under the French. Interviews, Skhirat and Marrakesh, June and July 1976.

tributed his entire salary among needy students. He was replaced after his death in March 1944 by 'Abd al-Qādir bin 'Alī al-Misfīwī, a man of learning whose father was a minister in the prior century under Sidi Hasan bin Muhammad. He was removed in August 1953 for protesting the king's deposition, and replaced briefly by Muhammad bin Hāshmī al-Misfīwī. After August 1953, the Scholarly Council continued only as a fiction. Upon his return to Morocco in November 1955, Sidi Muhammad bin Yusif dismissed both the rector and the controller.

French "organization" of the mosque-universities played a role in undermining the organizational basis of higher Islamic learning, but a more significant factor was the increasing availability beginning in the 1930s of government schools run by the French, which siphoned off the children of Morocco's elite. In a context analogous to what Colonna (1975) has described for Algeria, Islamic institutions became the least attractive option open to Moroccan Muslims in colonial society. Moreover, significant numbers of Moroccan graduates from French schools began by the 1930s to fill posts in the colonial bureaucracy and to play other key roles in colonial society that remained open to Muslims. Studies in a mosque-university ceased to be an effective means of social advancement.

The consequence was to leave the mosque-universities primarily to poor students of rural origin. Contemporary estimates of the number of students of rural and urban origin at the Qarawiyin indicate the significance of these changes. In 1924, 300 students were from Fez itself, whereas 419 were from outlying and predominantly rural regions (Marty 1924: 337). By 1938, only 100 students were from Fez and 800 were of rural origin (Berque 1938: 197). Although exact figures are unavailable for Marrakesh, consultants estimate that there were roughly 400 students at the Yusufiya in the early 1930s, of whom about 150 were from Marrakesh itself. The number of urban students had dropped to a handful by 1935, and almost none were from prominent rural or urban families. Islamic education had begun to be regarded with disdain even by those who took part in it during earlier periods because of the lack of "analysis and synthesis" in its style and content (Berque 1974: 173-179). Such a criticism implicitly compared the style and content of Islamic education with that at least ideally available in schools provided by the French.

In the first decade after colonial rule was established, concerned Moroccan bourgeoisie sought to meet the challenge of French-controlled education through the creation of "Free Schools" that were independent of French control but that adopted some European subjects and pedagogical methods to provide an alternative education, primarily in Arabic. These schools reached their maximum enrollments of 1,500-2,000 students in the mid-1920s, a significant figure since total Moroccan Muslim enrollment in French schools was about 6,000 in the same period, after which enrollments steadily declined (Damis 1973: 16). As important as such schools were as an ideological expression on the part of those who backed them, their long-term educational impact was minimal. Moroccan notables saw their children's futures and their own increasingly tied to the training and certification that only French schools could provide.

THE MORE interesting, and difficult, question is why this collapse had no direct impact upon the basic popular and learned paradigm of valued knowledge as fixed and memorizable, especially since at least in principle the social reproduction of such knowledge was necessary to make available the word of God for the guidance of the Islamic community. Why did the effective collapse not result in any major concerted action, or reaction, on the part of men of learning? This issue directly involves the relation of knowledge to society in the Moroccan context and the way in which value is placed on various bodies of knowledge and its carriers.

Traditionally educated Moroccan intellectuals were acutely aware of the major transformations that their society was experiencing as a consequence of colonial rule. In practical terms, the principal response of reformist intellectuals to this perceived crisis was merely to seek to persuade those who already possessed an understanding of the religious sciences to accept the "new orthodoxy" which they advocated. Yet many of these same individuals sent their sons and daughters, as did 'Abd ar-Rahman, to French-run schools rather than to mosque-universities or even the independent "Free Schools."

A partial explanation for the inaction of men of learning is that colonial rule posed no direct threat to their material interests. As with their nineteenth-century counterparts in British India (Metcalf 1982: 87-88), Morocco's men of learning realistically concluded that there was little effective resistance they could make against foreign rule, so sought instead to maintain their religious integrity. From the inception of the protectorate the French sought to engage the support of this elite by assimilating them into their system of indirect rule, a system that functioned with a high measure of success in the first two decades of colonial rule, especially under Lyautey (Rivet 1980). Unlike neighboring Algeria, where the influence of the traditional elite was systematically destroyed, the Moroccan traditional elite were given administrative and political preferment and their children were given access to French education. Despite radical political and economic transformations, the elite managed in general to confer their status upon their descendants (Leveau 1977; Waterbury 1970; cf. Bourdieu and Passeron 1977).

Taken by itself, an explanation based on material interests is insufficient. It does not account for the continued popular respect enjoyed by men of learning. In rural Morocco, religious intellectuals today are profoundly respected for the knowledge they possess even when as a body they did not actively participate in the nationalist and anticolonial movements. In Morocco's 1963 parliamentary elections, they constituted 130, or 57.4 percent, of the 223 candidates, and 27, or 55.2 percent, of the 49 actually elected (Leveau 1976: 188-189). A few traditionally educated intellectuals from prominent urban families, including 'Allal al-Fassi (see al-Fassi 1954; Rezette 1955; Waterbury 1970: 44) bridged the world of traditional learning and that of "liberal," European-style politics, but such transitions were exceptional. Most "ordinary" exemplars of mosque-university education regarded direct engagement in organized political activity as suspect and alien. Although their mistrust of political parties and plans for economic development have been characterized as based upon "a certain confused ideal of social justice" (Leveau 1976: 93), they enjoy extensive support among peasants and tribesmen, small landholders and shopkeepers.

The ideal of social justice held by traditional men of learning is "confused" only when analysts consider it in Western categories. Two implicit premises of the world view of traditionally educated Moroccan intellectuals have already been indicated—the notion of inequality as a natural fact of the social order and a highly restricted sense of social responsibility. These premises are perhaps most effectively delineated through comparison with two contrasting traditions of "gentlemanly" education, English and Chinese, which also possessed implicit notions of social inequality. Students of public schools in Victorian England were instilled with a sense of equity or "fair play," leadership, and public spirit which had its analogues in political life, whereas in China men of learning were considered to possess exemplary moral virtues that suited them for positions of authority (Wilkinson 1964; Weber 1958). There was no expectation in Morocco that Islamic men of learning should constitute an ideological vanguard, even in times of major social upheaval. They could on occasion serve as iconic expressions of popular sentiment, but there was no developed tradition in which they were able to shape these sentiments or guide the direction of social change.

The affinity between popular conceptions of valued knowledge and those conveyed in Islamic education explain the continuing popular legitimacy of such forms of knowledge and, at least in principle, of its carriers. What of the limitations of form of Islamic knowledge and its associated intellectual technology? The notion that the most valued knowledge was fixed by memorization in the first place limited the number of texts that any individual could "possess" thoroughly, just as did the notion that valued knowledge was accessible to all men of learning. A range of new materials could be introduced, but there was no value placed upon specialization in a given field of knowledge within this tradition of learning. The consequence was that innovations of content tended to suffer the same fate as innovations in societies without developed traditions of writing. Men of influence in the milieus of learning could to a limited extent introduce new materials, but innovations suggested by others had little chance of taking hold. Nor could specialized forms of knowledge proliferate, even the valued attempts to introduce mathematics and military technology in the nineteenth century (al-Manuni 1973). The body of valued knowledge shared by men of learning of any generation shifted over time, but it did not become more elaborate in form. There was no room in this tradition for disciplinary competences to be carved out and elaborated by smaller, specialized communities of men of learning. Moreover, since knowledge was considered to be fixed and memorizable, the central ideological problem was that of justifying any change of form or content in terms of its essential replication of past forms, instead of allowing an elaboration of form and content at least partially autonomous from generally accepted forms.

In the past, the memorizable truths of Islamic education were passed from generation to generation. With the collapse of Islamic education in the 1930s, this is no longer the case. To the present, this demise of the technology of intellectual reproduction has had no pronounced impact; as elsewhere, major changes in educational systems take a long time to have a widespread impact. The concept of knowledge as fixed and memorizable truths is still concretely demonstrated in Moroccan society by men who have memorized the Quran and its proper recitation, and associated texts are still mnemonically carried by the last generation of traditionally educated men of learning. Yet the number of individuals who are able to demonstrate "possession" of such knowledge is rapidly diminishing. One consequence is that the older generation of men of learning consider their younger replacements as essentially ignorant, knowing little of Islamic law beyond the bilingual French and Arabic handbooks prepared by the Ministry of Justice. The accuracy of this appraisal is not at issue here, but implied in it is the notion that their replacements are little more than bureaucratically appointed specialists who carry neither the authority nor the sense of legitimacy that they regard themselves as having possessed in the past. This notion appears largely to be popularly shared.

The shift of religious knowledge from that which is mnemonically possessed to material that can only be consulted in books suggests a major transformation in the nature of knowledge and its carriers. It may still be ideologically maintained that religious knowledge is memorizable and immutable, as is certainly the case for the word of God as recorded in the Quran, but the lack of concrete embodiment of this premise in the carriers of such knowledge indicates a major shift. This shift may not be consciously recognized, just as many Muslim intellectuals claim that the French colonial experience had little impact on the belief and practice of Islam, which from a sociological point of view is decidedly not the case (Eickelman 1974).

One consequence of this shift is that socially recognized carriers of religious learning are no longer confined to those who have studied accepted texts in circumstances equivalent to those of the mosque-universities, with their bias toward favoring members of the elite. Those who can interpret what Islam "really" is can now be of more variable social status than was the case when mnemonics were an essential element in the legitimacy of knowledge. The carriers of religious knowledge will increasingly be anyone who can claim a strong Islamic commitment, as is the case among many of the educated urban youth. Freed from mnemonic domination, religious knowledge can be delineated and interpreted in a more abstract and flexible fashion. A long apprenticeship under an established man of learning is no longer a necessary prerequisite to legitimizing one's own religious knowledge. Printed and mimeographed tracts and the clandestine dissemination of "lessons" on cassettes have begun to replace the mosque as the center for disseminating visions of Islam that challenge those offered by the state.

FROM MOSQUE-UNIVERSITY TO RELIGIOUS INSTITUTE

After Morocco's independence in 1956, the French were in some ways able to play a larger role in formulating Morocco's educational policies than they could in the protectorate. In 1955, only 25,000 new students entered the primary cycle. In the fall of 1956, 130,000 new students were enrolled (Dichter 1976: 127). Between 1912 and 1954, only 530 Moroccan Muslims passed both sections of the *baccalauréat* examination; in 1957, 13,374 baccalaureate degrees were awarded (Lacouture and Lacouture 1958: 248; Waterbury 1970: 84). The French widened educational opportunities after 1945, but mass education began only after independence.

Under French rule, education continued to be elitist, as it was in practice at the Qarawiyin and the Yusufiya. Educational standards were high, as they remained for the first few years after independence. Even holders of primary school certificates attained positions of responsibility. But because of its commitment to mass education, independent Morocco's educational budget was overextended from the start. In the late 1950s, local communities enthusiastically contributed money and labor to supplement government efforts (Dichter 1976: 127). Once it became evident that the linkage between socioeconomic opportunity and educational attainment had become weakened, however, popular enthusiasm for modern education precipitously declined. As one traditional scholar commented, the long-term consequence of French and independent Moroccan educational policy was to destroy traditional education—today officially called "original" education—without replacing it with a strong, workable "modern" system.[2]

Islamic higher education, although neglected in the years immediately after independence, never entirely disappeared. Since the late 1960s, it has received renewed official attention as the government recognizes the advantages of retaining control over it. To accommodate the traditionally educated, the government took over and in some cases established religious institutes (*ma'āhid al-Islāmiya*) at the secondary and postsecondary levels. Thus in 1938, religious education in Spanish Morocco was organized by the colonial government to include several provincial religious institutes (*ma'āhid ad-dīniya*), and after 1944 an Institute for Higher Religious Studies (Instituto Superior Religioso) in Tetouan (Valderrama 1956: 342-366). After independence, the Tetouan Institute was officially integrated into Morocco's national university system as the Faculty of Islamic Theology of the Qarawiyin University. Also integrated into the Qarawiyin were the Institute of Islamic Studies (now *Dār al-Ḥadīth al-Ḥasaniya*) in Rabat, responsible for the training of contemporary Islamic scholars. What remains of the Yusufiya is now officially called the Faculty of Arabic Language and Literature of the Qarawiyin in Marrakesh, with nineteen formally recognized faculty as of 1976 and 236 "undergraduates," of whom twenty-two are women (AFME 1976: 2). Other institutes, including Taroudant and Tamgrut (established in the precincts of the old religious lodge in 1982), operate roughly at a postprimary educational level.

---

[2] Thomas Dichter (1976), a former teacher in a Moroccan secondary school in the 1960s who subsequently returned to study it as an anthropologist, provides an excellent "insider" account of schooling and attitudes toward it. The French also maintain a network of private lycées, administered through the Mission Universitaire et Culturelle Française. These schools ostensibly are for the children of French citizens in Morocco, but most of their students are from the Moroccan elite. In addition, the various military and police services run their own academies for the equivalent of secondary and postsecondary education. Unlike their civilian counterparts, these schools are adequately funded and staffed and have suffered no known disruptions from protests or strikes.

Instruction is exclusively in Arabic (except for the Qarawiyin in Fez, where French is officially available as a foreign language). Most graduates end up teaching in government-sponsored Quranic schools. Unlike the Qarawiyin, where many teachers are currently drawn from other Arab countries because of earlier gaps in the training of religious scholars in Morocco, the faculty in Marrakesh are primarily Moroccan.

The last rector of the Yusufiya, appointed shortly after independence, was Raḥḥāl al-Farrūqī, who is now dean of the Faculty of Arabic Language and Literature in Marrakesh. Originally from Awlād Ḥammū of the Ahl Ghāba tribe of the Sraghna plain, he was born into a lineage that consolidated its local authority during the protectorate. His father hired a talib to supervise his studies, and the talib even accompanied his protégé to the Qarawiyin in the 1930s. Today he is head of Morocco's League of Ulama (ar-Rābiṭa al-'ulamā'), and is considered to be Morocco's foremost grammarian and traditional orator. His lectures are televised every Ramadan, with the king among those in attendance.

As disenchantment with modern education grew more widespread in the 1960s, the government sought to expand the role of "original" education. In 1968, the government mandated a year of Quranic schooling prior to admission to the primary school cycle. This move temporarily lessened pressure on public schools, which can accommodate only roughly half of all eligible students. It also reaffirmed government respect for original education and provided additional sinecures for the traditionally educated. Original education thus regained a modicum of respectability. But the "new" system of original education is not a straightforward resurrection of the old. To the extent that memorization still occurs, it is on the basis of mass production to a standard curriculum, complete with examinations, as opposed to the style of earlier institutions. It also systematically introduces students to the reading and writing of secular texts, something that traditional Quranic schools did not do.

PERSONAL CHOICES

When I asked 'Abd ar-Rahman why he did not encourage his own children to pursue religious studies, he responded quite simply that "times change" (*tbaddal al-waqt*). The circumstances ordained by God for the community of believers today are different from those in the past. The theme of the present-day world as defective, deteriorating, and corrupt, often casually invoked by 'Abd ar-Rahman, is not unique to his generation. It is characteristic of writings of Moroccan historians from at least the sixteenth century to the present (Lévi-Provençal 1922). A consequence of this stylized characterization of social reality is to accept as given the impermanence and provisionality of all human affairs. It discourages metaphysical reflection on how things might have been, reflections that would challenge what God had actually ordained, or how things ought to be. It encourages instead attention to perceiving the exact present state of social and political affairs (Eickelman 1976: 126-130; see also Waterbury 1972: 156-158).

All of 'Abd ar-Rahman's seven children received education in government schools. The eldest son was born in the early 1940s; the youngest in the mid-1960s. His eldest son entered primary school under the French and received a secondary degree after independence. In a pattern common with many Moroccans who completed secondary studies in the 1960s, he joined the administration rather than continue directly to higher studies, although his ministry subsequently sent him to France for advanced specialized training. 'Abd ar-Rahman's eldest daughter received a primary education in the late 1950s and early 1960s but, again in common with women of the period in smaller towns, where higher education was locally unavailable, she did not continue at the time. The qadi's younger daughter, who began primary studies in the late 1960s, is presently engaged in secondary studies. The other sons all studied through the secondary level. One is a senior manager for an investment firm in Casablanca; another is an

FIGURE 4. The Qadi in his Courtyard, 1969.

intermediate schoolteacher in Boujad and has been a member of the town's municipal council. A younger son was selected for the Palace school as a classmate for the crown prince.

CHALLENGES

Changes in basic patterns of thought and religiosity are often evident only in retrospect. As the late Raymond Aron (1970:

245) wrote, the main task of sociological explanation is "to render social or historical content more intelligible than it was in the experience of those who lived it." The implication of major changes in political and economic forms and in the intellectual technology of how ideas get reproduced and disseminated are just beginning to be explored in the context of Islamic and Middle Eastern studies.

One such "great transformation" is the introduction of literacy upon historically known and contemporary societies. Most of Jack Goody's *The Domestication of the Savage Mind* (1977) is concerned with the introduction of literacy in nonliterate societies. His discussion of the more nuanced problem of the shift from restricted to generalized literacy, from literacy possessed by a minority specialist elite to that accessible to wider elements of the population, occupies only the last ten pages of his book (1977: 152-162; see also Waldman 1985).

Şerif Mardin (1982a; 1982b) suggests the consequences of changes in styles of literacy and changes in the intellectual technology through which ideas are transmitted upon forms of religious knowledge and organization in his studies on the Turkish fundamentalist Saïd Nursi (1873-1960), the Bediüzzaman ("Nonpareil of the Times") and founder of the Nūr ("Light") movement. Through the nineteenth century, the accepted popular and elite notion was that religious knowledge and insight were acquired only with the guidance of a reputed master. In the Nur movement the "message" of the founder—his opinions on religious subjects and his commentaries on the Quran (written in Turkish, in itself a major innovation)—were more important than his person or personal ties to him. This aspect of the Nur movement was remarkably different from the practices of other Sufi orders. The form of Saïd Nursi's message was thus characterized by "the written text replacing the instructions of the charismatic leader and the attempt to make the central truths of the Koran intelligible to a wide audience" (Mardin 1982b: 19).

This style of religiosity was made possible by what Mardin terms the "communications revolution" that began to be felt in Turkey by the late nineteenth century. Patterns of governmental organization and authority changed substantially, as well as the forms in which knowledge and information were construed and communicated. Even when persons in authority thought they were using new technologies to preserve the old, new forms of thought and authority were shaped by the telegraph, newspapers, magazines, and an expanded (even if not mass) educational system. Newspapers and magazines, for instance, "replaced expostulation [with] arguments which were addressed to the presumed shared rationality of the readers" (Mardin 1982b: 13). The Nur movement spread with particular rapidity among the intelligentsia of Turkey's provincial centers: schoolteachers, functionaries, and others who were linked at least indirectly with the new communicative styles and who constituted the principal audience for the proliferation of newspapers and pamphlets.

An equivalent incipient "great transformation" of religiosity in Morocco may be the recent proliferation of loosely organized associations of Islamic militants who characterize themselves as "neo-Salafis," perhaps unaware that the same term was used by many men of learning in the 1930s, or even "the Muslims" (al-islamiyūn), in recognition of their self-proclaimed role of being the true carriers of Islam (Etienne and Tozy 1979: 245). The latter term also has a prior usage, known to professional historians in Morocco: in the late nineteenth century it referred to Jews who had converted to Islam.

The growth of these informal associations of young militants is linked to disenchantment with the results of over two decades of independence and an awareness of similar movements elsewhere in the Middle East. Interviews with participants in these groups, composed of students, schoolteachers, shopkeepers, and craftsmen, especially those living in the "popular" quarters of large towns in which recent rural emigrants predominate, suggest that they share a strong consciousness of social inequality, and a belief that the government will do little to ameliorate their situation. In their judgment, the government's objective is primarily to increase the wealth of the present political elite (Etienne and Tozy 1979: 251). Etienne and Tozy hypothesize that the growth of these associations is a "compensatory phenomenon." Independence in their view did not substantially improve the conditions of life in Morocco, so participants in the militant Islamic groups turn to renewed Islamic faith to avert "despair." For them, the dynamism associated in the past with independence is now associated with Islam.

The growth of Islamic militancy in Morocco is more than the displacement of unrealized hopes associated with independence. A stronger case can be made for interpreting the proliferation of these groups in the context of long-term changes in styles of religiosity more akin to those suggested by Goody and Mardin. Organizationally, the neo-Salafi groups bear superficial resemblance to the student groups prevalent during 'Abd ar-Rahman's years at the Yusufiya. Their formal organization is minimal, so that not all groups even have distinctive names. They seek to disseminate their ideas through discussions at accommodating mosques and in secondary schools. As with roughly analogous groups in Egypt, recruits are mainly educated youth of small town or village origin, politically aware and currently living in communities experiencing rapid urbanization (Ansari 1984: 132-134; Ibrahim 1980: 438). Proselytism is mainly through discreet personal contact. Unlike the religious groups of 'Abd ar-Rahman's generation or the early political groups of the 1930s, their supporters are not primarily culled from the sons (and, today, daughters) of the elite. They attract persons with some education who are unaffiliated to political parties, and their goal is to create a distinctly Islamic public opinion (Etienne and Tozy 1979: 248). Some receive modest financial support from fundamentalist groups elsewhere, notably Saudi Arabia, Pakistan, and Iraq. All deprecate the traditional religious orders as possessing a weak intellectual level, an argument that would appear to have been won long ago, at least among the educated. A more contemporary concern is their view of the "official" men of learning, those honored by the state, as "bought" men who have too readily acquiesced to the wishes of the monarch. Some attribute the monarchy with weakening the influence of the men of learning of the mosque-universities (evidently forgetting the role of the French), compelling them to endorse such non-Islamic practices as the clause in the Moroccan constitution that declares that succession to the monarchy is henceforth to be by male primogeniture (Hassan II 1978: 228). Some also interpret the appointment of a Syrian to head the Dar al-Hadith al-Hassaniya in Rabat as indicative of governmental efforts to circumscribe the role of Morocco's men of learning.

Another distinction by which Islamic militants distance themselves from the men of learning of 'Abd ar-Rahman's generation is their linkage between personal immorality, which is also roundly condemned by the older 'ulama, and the nature of the economic and political system, which is not (Yasin 1979). Some militants say that they are "preparing" for political action (Etienne and Tozy 1979: 255), an interesting phrase that presumably shielded them until recently from government interference. Yet the attitude of the state toward these groups has rapidly changed. It is significant that in the 1981 riots in Casablanca, no claims were made that Islamic militants played a major part. Perhaps because the monarchy itself relies upon religious legitimation, it has acted with caution in curbing these groups. At the time of Etienne and Tozy's study, their activities were monitored but not proscribed. That situation has now changed. After the January 1984 riots in Morocco, coinciding with the Islamic summit conference held in Casablanca, seventy-one arrests of Islamic militants were made. They were charged with incitement to rebellion and threats to internal security. Some of those charged allegedly possessed photographs of key officials, in order to identify them for kidnaping or assassination (Mekki 1984). The evidence presented by the prosecution failed to convince outside observers at the trial. The handling of the case and the severity of the sentences imposed, including thirteen death sentences, indicates the severity with which the government views the challenge posed by Islamic militants.

One of the most important new elements in Islamic militancy in Morocco is a sharp break with the past tradition of reliance upon authoritative commentary from qualified men of learning. Militants assert implicitly that each Muslim can personally judge whether the state, the monarch, and the "official" men of learning act in accord with the precepts of Islam. This attitude is less a challenge to the monarchy than to the religious monopoly of "official" Islamic spokesmen (Etienne and Tozy 1979: 244, 259). The notion that Muslims can directly interpret their faith without reliance upon intermediaries represents a significant break with the past, one made feasible by greater access to an educational system freed from direct ties to official orthodoxy.

There is growing disenchantment with the monarchy, some of which has been openly expressed, if with caution. Nonetheless, the fragmented associations of Islamic militants have yet to widen their respective bases of support outside major urban centers. The religious attitudes represented by traditional men of learning sustain widespread support in large part because the carriers of competing attitudes, however perceptive they may be in their analysis of some of Morocco's political, social, and economic problems, have not yet managed to find a resonance in popular understandings of the linkage between Islam and politics. Unlike Iran, where the religious establishment has had an organized financial base largely autonomous from government control, a tradition of opposition to secular authority, and a monarchy that never directly claimed religious legitimacy as one of its central tenets, the Moroccan monarch continues to be regarded by the "silent majority" in the countryside as "God's deputy on earth" (khalīfat Allāh fī-l-'arḍ). Morocco's religious "establishment" does not possess an organized financial base independent from political authority, so that even the possibility of independent oppositional action is seriously circumscribed. Nor is there the popular expectation that royal authority and religious authority are meant to be autonomous. The prevalent popular notion of the monarch as God's deputy is rarely invoked among the educated, even supporters of the monarchy, but indicates the presumption of religious legitimacy with which any self-consciously Islamic or political opposition must contend.

Any society contains competing discourses, which are not internally consistent and are filled with tensions and ambiguities. In Morocco, these competing voices are unequally weighted. Activists in organized political groups and Islamic militants each seek a departure from the accepted status quo. As such they must consciously articulate and win acceptance for wide-ranging reorientations toward politics and society. In contrast, Morocco's men of learning can draw upon the mainstream of existing implicit acceptance of what Karl Mannheim calls "enduring actuality as compared with the progressive desire for change," a preference for "organic," existing social units rather than "classes," and above all an emphasis upon concreteness in its discussion of politics and society (Mannheim 1971: 172). Advocates of change from the status quo must fully articulate their intentions in seeking to win support.

Men of learning, by accepting existing social and religious arrangements, can presume support without fully elaborating the ideological basis of their actions. Thomas S. Kuhn, analyzing changing support for scientific paradigms, argues that scientists who have invested their training and entire productive careers in a certain way of doing things often resist or place little value on newer approaches. They are confident that "the older paradigm will ultimately solve all its problems, that nature can be shoved into the box the paradigm provides" (Kuhn 1962: 150). Applied to the Moroccan case, the analogy of Morocco's traditional men of learning with Kuhn's scientific communities is only partial. The scientific community as described by Kuhn is more closed and self-contained, while the strength, and limitation, of Morocco's men of learning is the extent to which they articulate the views of a majority of the population, even if they are not the political activists. The conservative thought represented by Morocco's men of learning survives in part because its supporters move in separate grooves from those civil servants, educated youth, and others caught in Morocco's "modern" sector. Within these categories of Morocco's population, popular support for a more traditional intellectual and religious style has waned. Competing styles of religious thought and action have begun to emerge. In Iran, the organization and ideology of the religious establishment remained autonomous in spite of vigorous efforts by the state to curb its influence prior to the revolution. Morocco's traditional men of learning have had neither the independent base nor the organization to pose a political challenge. They continue to benefit from state patronage, but the state-sponsored centers of religious learning are not producing a new generation capable of exercising religious leadership of a scope comparable to that of an older, disappearing generation. The fact of competing voices of Islam, some of which claim to be more "authentic" than the others, is not in itself new to Morocco or to other parts of the Islamic world. At the pinnacle of Moroccan society, key traditional religious leaders continue to have royal patronage and access to state-controlled radio and television. Increasingly absent, however, are the complex local expressions of traditional learning and the persons to maintain it. Traditional learning and its carriers in the past stood outside the political arena. It is unlikely that its successors will continue to follow this particular aspect of tradition.

GLOSSARY

The second of two forms indicates the plural. Transcription is according to local usage unless otherwise indicated.

'adl: Notary.

'ālim; *'ulamā*: Religious scholar.

'āmmī; *'awām*: Common; ordinary.

bakāns: Emigrant worker; from French *vacance*.

baraka: Supernatural blessing; abundance.

bay'a: Oath of fealty.

bid'a: Innovation.

da'wa: Personal prayer.

ḍāhir: Royal decree.

dawwār: Rural local community.

dīr: Piedmont.

fahm: Understanding.

fitna: Sedition.

fqīh; *fuqahā*: An Islamic jurist; a Quranic teacher; a literate person (now archaic).

ḥābūs; *aḥbās*: Pious endowment.

ḥāfiḍ: A major scholar; a person who has memorized the entire Quran. Literary usage, *ḥāfiz*.

ḥājj: The pilgrimage to Mecca; also an honorific title used by those who have made the pilgrimage.

ḥaram: Forbidden; religiously impure.

ḥizb: One of the sixty divisions of the Quran for recitational purposes.

ijāza: Teaching license.

'ilm; *'ulūm*: Religious knowledge or scholarship.

imām: Prayer leader; leader of the faithful.

jāmi'a: Mosque-university; mosque.

jallāba: Tunic.

kātib: Clerk or scribe.

khalīfa: Deputy.

khāṣṣa: elite, special.

khuṭba: Friday sermon.

laṭīf: Collective prayer in time of distress.

madīna: City; in North Africa this term often specifically designates the precolonial part of a city.

madrasa: Place of study; a school; hostel for religious students.

ma'had; *ma'āhid*: Institute.

Makhzan: Moroccan government; lit. "strongbox."

mālik: King.

marabout: A person, living or dead, thought to have a special relation toward God which enables him or her to ask for God's grace on behalf of clients and to communicate it to them. See also *ṣāliḥ*.

ma'rūf: Known; socially recognized.

mqaddam: Spokesman (used in a variety of contexts); minor government official.

msīd: Quranic school.

nāḍir: Overseer. Literary usage, *nāẓir*.

nās khāṣṣa: Lit. "special" people; the elite.

niẓām: Organization; order.

qāḍī; *quḍā*: A religious judge.

qāid: Tribal chief or leader appointed over a tribe or small town during the protectorate; now an official of the Ministry of the Interior responsible for a rural or urban administrative unit. Literary usage, *qā'id*.

qā'ida; qawā'id: "The way things are done."

'qāl: Reason.

qasam: Oath.

qaṣīda: A verse form.

qrīb: "Close."

rasm: Property title.

Salafī: Reformist Muslim.

ṣāliḥ: A pious or devout person; a saint; in some contexts, a marabout.

ṣdāq: Bridewealth.

shaykh: Religious teacher or head of a mystic order; government official.

shrā': Islamic law (with definite article); straight path. Classical usage: *sharī'a*.

shrīf; shurfā: Patrilineal descendant of the Prophet Muhammad through his daughter, Fatima. Literary usage, *sharīf*.

sība: Anarchy; dissidence.

siḥr: Magic.

silka: A recitational quarter of the Quran (lit. "thread").

ṣulḥ: Truce.

sulṭa: Authority.

tafsīr: Quranic exegesis.

ṭā'ifa: Group; sect; faction.

ṭālib; ṭulbā: Religious student; scholar.

tarjama; tarājim: Traditional biography or autobiography.

tᶜarqība: The sacrifice of a bull or bulls to conclude or renew an oath of allegiance or to seek a truce.

tartīb: Rural tax on herds and crops established by the French in Morocco.

tashalḥīt: One of the three major Berber languages spoken in Morocco.

ᶜushūr: Islamic tithe.

zāwiya: Religious lodge or residence of a prominent marabout.

BIBLIOGRAPHY

Abu-Lughod, Janet L. *Rabat: Urban Apartheid in Morocco*. Princeton: Princeton University Press, 1980.

Abun-Nasr, Jamil M. "The Salafiyya Movement in Morocco: The Religious Bases of the Moroccan Nationalist Movement," *St. Antony's Papers* 16 (1963): 90-105.

Adam, André. *Casablanca*. Paris: Editions du Centre National de la Recherche Scientifique, 1968.

AFME (American Friends of the Middle East). "Institutional Report: Qarawiyin University." Washington: AFME, 1976.

Akhavi, Shahrough. *Religion and Politics in Contemporary Iran*. Albany: State University of New York Press, 1980.

Ansari, Hamied N. "The Islamic Militants in Egyptian Politics," *International Journal of Middle East Studies* 16 (1984): 123-144.

Ariès, Philippe. *Centuries of Childhood*. New York: Vintage Books, 1962.

Aron, Raymond. *Main Currents in Sociological Thought*, vol. 2, translated by Richard Howard and Helen Weaver. Garden City: Doubleday Anchor, 1970.

Aubin, Eugène [Descos]. *Morocco of To-Day*. London: J. M. Dent and Co., 1906.

Ayache, Germain. *Etudes d'histoire marocaine*. Rabat: Société Marocaine des Editeurs Réunis, 1979.

Baer, Gabriel, ed. *The 'Ulamā' in Modern History*. Jerusalem: Israel Oriental Society, 1971.

Bailyn, Bernard. *Education in the Forming of American Society*. New York: Vintage Books, 1960.

Becker, Anton L., and Aram Yengoyan, eds. *The Imagination of Reality: Essays in Southeast Asian Coherence Systems*. Norwood, N.J.: Ablex, 1979.

Bernard, Stéphane. *The Franco-Moroccan Conflict, 1943-1956*. New Haven and London: Yale University Press, 1968.

Berque, Jacques. "Dans le Maroc nouveau: Le rôle d'une université islamique," *Annales d'Histoire Economique et Sociale* 10 (1938): 193-207.

―――. "Ville et université, aperçu sur l'histoire de l'école de Fès," *Revue Historique de Droit Français et Etranger* 27 (1949): 64-117.

―――. *Structures sociales du Haut-Atlas.* Paris: Presses Universitaires de France, 1955.

―――. *Al-Yousi: Problèmes de la culture marocaine au XVIIème siècle.* Paris and The Hague: Mouton, 1958.

―――. "Lieux et moments du réformisme Islamique." In *Maghreb: Histoire et sociétés*, pp. 162-188. Paris: Editions J. Duculot, 1974.

―――, and Julien Couleau. "Vers le modernisation du fellah marocain," *Bulletin Economique et Social du Maroc* 7 (1946): 18-25.

Berriau, Colonel. *L'officier de renseignements au Maroc.* Rabat: Imprimerie, Service de Renseignements, 1918.

Bidwell, Robin. *Morocco under Colonial Rule.* London: Frank Cass, 1973.

Binsaʿīd, Saʿīd. "Al-muthaqqaf al-makhzanī wa-taḥdīth ad-dawla: Bidāyāt as-salafiyya al-jadīda fī-l-maghrib," *al-Mustaqbal al-ʿArabī* (Beirut), no. 58 (December 1983): 27-38.

Bloch, Maurice. "Introduction." In *Political Language and Oratory in Traditional Society*, edited by Maurice Bloch, pp. 1-28. London and New York: Academic Press, 1975.

Bourdieu, Pierre. "Systems of Education and Systems of Thought," *International Social Science Journal* 19 (1967): 338-358.

―――. "Cultural Reproduction and Social Reproduction." In *Knowledge, Education and Cultural Change*, edited by Richard Brown, pp. 71-112. London: Tavistock Publications, 1973.

―――, and Jean-Claude Passeron. *Reproduction in Education, Society and Culture.* Beverly Hills: Sage Publications, 1977.

Brown, Kenneth. "Profile of a Nineteenth-Century Moroccan Scholar." In *Scholars, Saints, and Sufis*, edited by Nikki R. Keddie, pp. 127-148. Berkeley and Los Angeles: University of California Press, 1972.

―――. "The Impact of the *Dahir Berbère* in Salé." In *Arabs and Berbers*, edited by Ernest Gellner and Charles Micaud, pp. 201-215. London: Duckworth, 1973.

―――. *People of Salé: Tradition and Change in a Moroccan City, 1830-1930.* Cambridge: Harvard University Press, 1976.

Brown, Leon Carl. "The Religious Establishment in Husainid Tunisia." In *Scholars, Saints, and Sufis,* edited by Nikki R. Keddie, pp. 47-91. Berkeley and Los Angeles: University of California Press, 1972.

Brunel, René. *Le monachisme errant dans l'Islam.* Paris: Librairie Larose, 1955.

Bulliet, Richard. *The Patricians of Nishapur.* Cambridge: Harvard University Press, 1972.

Burke, Edmund, III. "The Moroccan Ulama, 1860-1912: An Introduction." In *Scholars, Saints, and Sufis,* edited by Nikki R. Keddie, pp. 93-125. Berkeley and Los Angeles: University of California Press, 1972.

————. *Prelude to Protectorate in Morocco.* Chicago: University of Chicago Press, 1976.

Castries, H. de. "Les sept patrons de Merrakech," *Hespéris* 4 (1924): 245-303.

Cénival, Pierre de. "La légende du juif Ibn Mech'al et la fête du sultan des tolba à Fès," *Hespéris* 5 (1925): 137-218.

Christelow, Alan. "The Muslim Judge in Algeria and Senegal," *Comparative Studies in Society and History* 24 (1982): 3-24.

Cimetière, J. "Notice sur Bou Djad," *Revue du Monde Musulman* 24 (1913): 277-289.

Cohn, Bernard S. "Anthropology and History in the 1980s," *Journal of Interdisciplinary History* 12 (1981): 227-252.

Colonna, Fanny. *Instituteurs algériens, 1883-1939.* Paris: Presses de la Fondation Nationale des Sciences Politiques, 1975.

Crapanzano, Vincent. *The Hamadsha: A Study in Moroccan Ethnopsychiatry.* Berkeley and Los Angeles: University of California Press, 1973.

————. *Tuhami: Portrait of a Moroccan.* Chicago: University of Chicago Press, 1980.

Damis, John. "Early Moroccan Reactions to the French Protectorate: The Cultural Dimension," *Humaniora Islamica* 1 (1973): 15-31.

Davis, Susan Schaefer. *Patience and Power: Women's Lives in a Moroccan Village.* Cambridge: Schenkman Publishing Co., 1983.

Delphin, Gaëtan. *Fas, son université et l'enseignement supérieur musulman.* Paris: Ernest Leroux, 1889.

Deverdun, Gaston. *Marrakesh des origines à 1912.* Rabat: Editions Techniques Nord-Africaines, 1959, 1966.

Dichter, Thomas. "The Problem of How to Act on an Undefined Stage: An Exploration of Culture, Change, and Individual Consciousness in the Moroccan Town of Sefrou—With a Focus on Three Modern Schools." Unpublished Ph.D. Dissertation in Anthropology, University of Chicago, December 1976.

Douglas, Mary. *Natural Symbols.* New York: Vintage Books, 1973.

Doutté, Edmond. "La Khot'ba burlesque de la fête des t'olba au Maroc." In *Recueil de Mémoires et de Textes,* 14th Congress of Orientalists, pp. 197-219. Algiers: A. Jourdan, 1905.

——. *En tribu.* Paris: Geuthner, 1914.

Durkheim, Emile. *The Elementary Forms of the Religious Life,* translated by Joseph Swain. London: Allen and Unwin, 1915.

——. *The Evolution of Educational Thought,* translated by Peter Collins. London: Routledge and Kegan Paul, 1977.

Dwyer, Kevin. *Moroccan Dialogues: Anthropology in Question.* Baltimore: Johns Hopkins University Press, 1982.

Eickelman, Dale F. *Moroccan Islam: Tradition and Society in a Pilgrimage Center.* Austin and London: University of Texas Press, 1976.

——. *The Middle East: An Anthropological Approach.* Englewood Cliffs N.J.: Prentice-Hall, Inc., 1981.

——. "Religion and Trade in Western Morocco," *Research in Economic Anthropology* 5 (1983): 335-348.

Escallier, Robert. *Citadins et espace urbain au Maroc.* Poitiers: Centre Interuniversitaire d'Etudes Méditerranéennes, 1981.

Etienne, Bruno, and Mohamed Tozy. "Le glissement des obligations Islamiques vers le phenomène associatif à Casablanca." *Annuaire de l'Afrique du Nord* 18 (1979): 235-259.

Evans-Pritchard, E. E. *The Nuer.* Oxford: Oxford University Press, 1940.

Fassi, 'Allal al-. *The Independence Movements in Arab North Africa,* translated by Hazem Zaki Nuseibeh. Washington: American Council of Learned Societies, 1954.

Fischer, Michael M. J. *Iran: From Religious Dispute to Revolution.* Cambridge: Harvard University Press, 1980a.

——. "Becoming Mollah: Reflections on Iranian Clerics in a Revolutionary Age," *Iranian Studies* 13 (1980b): 83-117.

——. "Islam and the Revolt of the Petit Bourgeoisie," *Daedalus* 111 (Winter 1982): 101-125.

French Protectorate, Morocco, Direction Générale de l'Instruction Publique. *Historique (1912-1930).* Rabat: Ecole du Livre, 1931.

Geertz, Clifford. *The Social History of an Indonesian Town*. Cambridge: The M.I.T. Press, 1965.

———. *Islam Observed*. New Haven and London: Yale University Press, 1968.

———. "Thinking as a Moral Act: Ethical Dimensions of Anthropological Fieldwork in the New States," *Antioch Review* 28 (1968b): 139-158.

———. "Suq: The Bazaar Economy in Sefrou." In *Meaning and Order in Moroccan Society*, by Clifford Geertz, Hildred Geertz, and Lawrence Rosen, pp. 123-313. New York and Cambridge: Cambridge University Press, 1979.

———. *Local Knowledge: Further Essays in Interpretive Anthropology*. New York: Basic Books, 1983.

———, Hildred Geertz, and Lawrence Rosen. *Meaning and Order in Moroccan Society*. New York and Cambridge: Cambridge University Press, 1979.

Geertz, Hildred. "A Statistical Profile of the Population of the Town of Sefrou in 1960: Analysis of the Census." In *Meaning and Order in Moroccan Society*, by Clifford Geertz, Hildred Geertz, and Lawrence Rosen, pp. 393-506. New York and Cambridge: Cambridge University Press, 1979.

Gellner, Ernest. "Patterns of Rural Rebellion in Morocco during the Early Years of Independence." In *Arabs and Berbers*, edited by Ernest Gellner and Charles Micaud, pp. 361-374. London: Duckworth, 1973 (original 1962).

Goody, Jack. *The Domestication of the Savage Mind*. Cambridge: Cambridge University Press, 1977.

Gramschi, Antonio. "The Intellectuals." In *Selections from the Prison Notebooks*, edited and translated by Quentin Hoare and Geoffrey Nowell Smith, pp. 3-43. New York: International Publishers, 1971.

Green, Arnold H. "Political Attitudes and Activities of the Ulama in the Liberal Age: Tunisia as an Exceptional Case," *International Journal of Middle East Studies* 7 (1976): 209-241.

———. *The Tunisian Ulama, 1873-1915*. Leiden: E. J. Brill, 1978.

Griaule, Marcel. *Conversations with Ogotêmmeli*. London: Oxford University Press for the International African Institute, 1965 (original 1948).

Hammoudi, Abdellah. "Aspects de la mobilisation populaire à la campagne vus à travers la biographie d'un mahdi mort en 1919." In *Islam et politique au Maghreb*, edited by Ernest Gellner and

Jean-Claude Vatin, pp. 47-55. Paris: Centre National de la Recherche Scientifique, 1981.

Hart, David Montgomery. *The Aith Waryaghar of the Moroccan Rif: An Ethnography and History*. Tucson: University of Arizona Press, 1976.

Hassan II. *The Challenge*, translated by Anthony Rhodes. London: Macmillan, 1978.

Heyworth-Dunne, J. *An Introduction to the History of Education in Modern Egypt*. London: Frank Cass, 1968.

Hodgson, Marshall. *The Venture of Islam*, Vol. I. Chicago: University of Chicago Press, 1974.

Hourani, Albert. "Ottoman Reform and the Politics of Notables." In *The Beginnings of Modernization in the Middle East: The Nineteenth Century*, edited by William R. Polk and Richard L. Chambers, pp. 41-68. Chicago: University of Chicago Press, 1968.

————. *Arabic Thought in the Liberal Age, 1798-1939*. Revised ed. New York: Oxford University Press, 1970.

Hussein, Taha. *The Stream of Days*, translated by Hilary Waymont. London: Longman, Green and Co., 1948.

Ibn Khaldun. *The Muqaddimah*, translated by Franz Rosenthal. 2nd ed. Princeton: Princeton University Press, 1967.

Ibrahim, Saad Eddin. "Anatomy of Egypt's Militant Islamic Groups," *International Journal of Middle East Studies* 12 (1980): 423-453.

Jemma, D. *Les tanneurs de Marrakech*. Algiers: Centre Nationale de la Recherche Scientifique, 1972.

Jirārī, 'Abd Allāh. *Al-Muḥaddith al-ḥāfiẓ Abū Shu'ayb ad-Dukkālī*. Jadida and Casablanca: Al-Najāḥ Press, 1976.

Julien, Charles-André. *L'Afrique du nord en marche*, 3rd ed. Paris: Julliard, 1972.

Kane, Hamidou. *Ambiguous Adventure*. New York: Walker and Company, 1963.

Keddie, Nikki R., ed. *Scholars, Saints, and Sufis*. Berkeley and Los Angeles: University of California Press, 1972.

Kessler, Clive S. *Islam and Politics in a Malay State*. Ithaca and London: Cornell University Press, 1978.

Kuhn, Thomas S. *The Structure of Scientific Revolutions*. Chicago: University of Chicago Press, 1962.

Lacouture, Jean, and Simone Lacouture. *La Maroc à l'épreuve*. Paris: Editions du Seuil, 1958.

Lapidus, Ira Marvin. *Muslim Cities in the Later Middle Ages*. Cambridge: Harvard University Press, 1967.

Laroui, Abdallah. *L'idéologie arabe contemporaine*. Paris: François Maspéro, 1967.

————. *The Crisis of Arab Intellectuals*. Berkeley and Los Angeles: University of California Press, 1974.

————. *The History of the Maghrib: An Interpretive Essay*, translated by Ralph Mannheim. Princeton: Princeton University Press, 1977a (original 1970).

————. *Les origines sociales et culturelles du nationalisme marocain (1830-1912)*. Paris: François Maspéro, 1977b.

Leo Africanus. *The History and Description of Africa*, translated by John Pory. London: Hakluyt Society, 1896 (original 1526).

Le Tourneau, Roger. *Fès avant le protectorat*. Casablanca: Société Marocaine de Librairie et d'Edition, 1949.

————. *Evolution politique de l'Afrique du Nord musulmane, 1920-1961*. Paris: Librairie Armand Colin, 1962.

Leveau, Rémy. *Le fellah marocain: Defenseur du trône*. Paris: Presses de la Fondation Nationale des Sciences Politiques, 1976.

————. "The Rural Elite as an Element in the Social Stratification of Morocco." In *Commoners, Climbers and Notables*, edited by C. A. O. van Nieuwenhuijze, pp. 226-247. Leiden: E. J. Brill, 1977.

Lévy-Provençal, E. *Les Historiens des chorfa*. Paris: Librairie Orientaliste Paul Geuthner, 1922.

Lewis, Oscar. *The Children of Sanchez: Autobiography of a Mexican Family*. New York: Random House, 1961.

Lienhardt, Godfrey. *Divinity and Experience: The Religion of the Dinka*. Oxford: Clarendon Press, 1967.

McLachlan, James. "The *Choice of Hercules*: American Student Societies in the Early 19th Century." In *The University in Society*, edited by Lawrence Stone, pp. 449-494. Princeton: Princeton University Press, 1974.

Maher, Vanessa. *Women and Property in Morocco*. Cambridge: Cambridge University Press, 1974.

Makdisi, George. *The Rise of Colleges: Institutions of Learning in Islam and the West*. Edinburgh: Edinburgh University Press, 1981.

Mannheim, Karl. "Conservative Thought." In *From Karl Mannheim*, edited by Kurt H. Wolff, pp. 132-222. New York: Oxford University Press, 1971.

Manūnī, Muḥammad al-. *Maẓāhir yuqẓa al-Maghrib al-ḥadīth*, part 1. Rabat: Omnia Press, 1973.

Marais, Octave. "Les relations entre la monarchie et la classe dirigeante au Maroc," *Revue Française de Science Politique* 19 (1969): 1172-1186.

Mardin, Serif. "Bediüzzaman Said Nursi (1873-1960): The Shaping of a Vocation." In *Religious Organization and Religious Experience*, edited by John Davis, pp. 65-79. London: Academic Press, 1982a.

————. "Bediüzzaman Saïd Nursi: Preliminary Approaches to the Biography of a Turkish Muslim Fundamentalist Thinker." Manuscript, 1982b (cited with permission of the author).

Marty, Paul. "L'Université de Qaraouiyne," *Renseignements Coloniaux, Supplément de l'Afrique Française*, November 1924, pp. 329-353.

Massignon, Louis. *The Passion of al-Hallāj*, translated by Herbert Mason. Princeton: Princeton University Press, 1982 (original 1922).

Mauss, Marcel. "Essai sur les variations saisonnières des sociétés eskimos: Etude de morphologie sociale." In *Sociologie et Anthropologie*, edited by Marcel Mauss, pp. 389-477. Paris: Presses Universitaires de France, 1966.

Maxwell, Gavin. *Lords of the Atlas*. London: Longmans, 1966.

Mekki, Aïcha. "Procès des extrémistes de Casablanca," *L'Opinion* (Rabat), July 27, 1984, p. 4.

Merad, Ali. *Le réformisme musulman en Algérie de 1925 à 1940*. Paris and The Hague: Mouton, 1967.

————. *Ibn Badis: Commentateur du Coran*. Paris: Librairie Orientaliste Paul Geuthner, 1971.

Merton, Robert K. "Insiders and Outsiders: A Chapter in the Sociology of Knowledge," *American Journal of Sociology* 78 (1972): 9-47.

Metcalf, Barbara Daly. *Islamic Revival in British India: Deoband, 1860-1900*. Princeton: Princeton University Press, 1982.

Michaux-Bellaire, E. "L'enseignement indigène au Maroc," *Revue du Monde Musulman* 15 (1911): 422-452.

Montagne, Robert. "Un essai de régionalisme au Maroc." Archives du Centre des Hautes Etudes de l'Administration Musulmane (Paris), 451. Manuscript, 1941.

Monteil, Vincent. "Les bureaux arabes au Maghreb (1833-1961)," *Esprit*, November 1961, pp. 575-606.

Mosca, Gaetano. *The Ruling Class: Elementi di Scienza Politica,* translated by Hannah D. Kahn. New York: McGraw Hill, 1939.

Mottahedeh, Roy P. "Review of Bulliet, *The Patricians of Nishapur,*" *Journal of the American Oriental Society* 95 (1975): 491-495.

————. *Loyalty and Leadership in an Early Islamic Society.* Princeton: Princeton University Press, 1980.

Mouliéras, Auguste. *Le Maroc inconnu. I. Exploration du Rif.* Paris: Librairie Coloniale, 1895.

————. *Le Maroc inconnu. II. Exploration des Djebala.* Paris: Augustin Challamel, 1899.

Munson, Henry, Jr. *The House of Si Abd Allah.* New Haven: Yale University Press, 1984.

Noin, Daniel. *La population rurale du Maroc.* Paris: Presses Universitaires de France, 1970.

Notopoulos, James A. "Mnemosyne in Oral Literature," *Transactions and Proceedings of the American Philological Association* 69 (1938): 465-493.

Ong, Walter J. *Orality and Literacy: The Technologizing of the Word.* London and New York: Methuen, 1981.

Pascon, Paul. *Le Haouz de Marrakech.* Rabat: Centre Universitaire de la Recherche Scientifique, 1977.

Péretié, A. "Les medrasas de Fès," *Archives Marocaines* 18 (1912): 257-372.

Rabinow, Paul. *Symbolic Domination: Cultural Form and Historical Change in Morocco.* Chicago: University of Chicago Press, 1975.

Radin, Paul. *Primitive Man as a Philosopher.* New York: Dover Books, 1957 (original 1927).

Reynolds, L. D. and N. G. Wilson. *Scribes and Scholars: A Guide to the Transmission of Greek and Latin Literature.* Oxford: Clarendon Press, 1974.

Rezette, Robert. *Les partis politiques marocains.* Paris: Librairie Armand Colin, 1955.

Ricard, Prosper. *Le Maroc (Les Guides Bleus),* 4th ed. Paris: Librairie Hachette, 1930.

Rivet, Daniel. "Lyautey l'africain," *L'Histoire,* no. 29 (December 1980): 17-24.

Rosen, Lawrence. "Social Identity and Points of Attachment: Approaches to Social Organization." In Clifford Geertz, Hildred Geertz, and Lawrence Rosen, *Meaning and Order in Moroccan*

Society, pp. 19-111. New York and Cambridge: Cambridge University Press, 1979.

———. "Equity and Discretion in a Modern Islamic Legal System," *Law and Society Review* 15 (1980-1981): 217-245.

Rosenthal, Franz. *Knowledge Triumphant: The Concept of Knowledge in Mediaeval Islam*. Leiden: E. J. Brill, 1970.

Roulleaux-Dugage, Georges. *Lettres du Maroc*. Paris: Plon-Nourrit, 1915.

Saad, Elias N. *Social History of Timbuktu: The Role of Muslim Scholars and Notables, 1400-1900*. New York: Cambridge University Press, 1983.

Schumpeter, Joseph A. *Capitalism, Socialism and Democracy*. 3rd ed. New York: Harper & Row, 1962 (original 1950).

Schuyler, Philip D. "Music Education in Morocco: Three Models," *The World of Music* (Berlin) 21: 3 (1979): 19-31.

Shils, Edward. *The Intellectuals and the Powers*. Chicago and London: University of Chicago Press, 1972.

———. *Tradition*. Chicago and London: University of Chicago Press, 1981.

Simmel, Georg. *The Sociology of Georg Simmel*, translated and edited by Kurt H. Wolff. New York: Free Press, 1964.

Sivan, Emmanuel. "Ibn Taymiyya: Father of the Islamic Revolution," *Encounter* 60, (May 1983): 41-50.

Snouck Hurgronje, Christiaan. *Mekka in the Latter Part of the 19th Century*. Leiden: E. J. Brill, 1931.

Sūsī, Mukhtār as-. *Al-Ma'sūl*. Casablanca: Al-Najāḥ Press, 1961.

Tawfīq, Aḥmad. *Al-Mujtama' al-maghribī fī al-qarn at-tās' 'ashar: Inūltān, 1850-1912*. 2nd ed. Casablanca: al-Najāḥ Press, 1983.

Touimi, Mohammed Benjelloun, Abdelkebir Khatibi, and Mohammad Kably, eds. *Ecrivains marocains du protectorat à 1965*. Paris: Sindbad, 1974.

Turner, Victor. *The Forest of Symbols: Aspects of Ndembu Ritual*. Ithaca: Cornell University Press, 1967 (essay originally published in 1959).

'Uthmān, Muḥammad ibn. *Al-jāmi'a al-Yūsufīya bi-Marrākush*. Cairo: Economical Press, 1935.

Valderrama Martínez, Fernando. *Historia de la acción cultural de España en Marruecos (1912-1956)*. Tetouan: Editora Marroquí, 1956.

Wagner, Daniel. "Memories of Morocco: The Influence of Age,

Schooling, and Environment on Memory," *Cognitive Psychology* 10 (1978): 1-28.

———. "Indigenous Education and Literacy in the Third World." In *Child Development and International Development: Research-Policy Interfaces*, edited by Daniel A. Wagner, pp. 77-86. San Francisco: Jossey-Bass, 1983.

———, and Abdelhamid Lotfi. "Traditional Islamic Education in Morocco: Sociohistorical and Psychological Perspectives," *Comparative Education Review* 24 (1980): 238-251.

Waldman, Marilyn R. "Primitive Mind/Modern Mind: New Approaches to an Old Problem Applied to Religion." In *Islam and the History of Religions: Perspectives on the Study of a Religious Tradition*, edited by Richard Martin. Tucson: University of Arizona Press, 1985 (in press).

Waterbury, John. *The Commander of the Faithful: The Moroccan Political Elite*. New York: Columbia University Press, 1970.

———. *North for the Trade: The Life and Times of a Berber Merchant*. Berkeley and Los Angeles: University of California Press, 1972.

Wattier. "Le carnaval de Marrakech," *France-Maroc*, July 15, 1919, pp. 3-8.

Weber, Max. "The Chinese Literati." In *From Max Weber: Essays in Sociology*, edited by H. H. Gerth and C. Wright Mills, pp. 416-444. New York: Oxford University Press, 1958.

Wilkinson, Rupert. *The Prefects: British Leadership and the Public School Tradition*. New York: Oxford University Press, 1964.

Yasin, Abd Assalam. *La révolution à l'heure de l'Islam*. Marseille: Presses de l'Imprimerie du Collège, 1979.

Yates, Francis A. *The Art of Memory*. Chicago: University of Chicago Press, 1966.

Young, Michael W. "Our Name is Women: We are Bought with Limesticks and Limepots: An Analysis of the Autobiographical Narrative of a Kalauna Woman," *Man*, new series 18 (1983): 478-501.

Zerdoumi, Nefissa. *Enfant d'hier*. Paris: François Maspéro, 1970.

INDEX

With the exception of *'ulamā'* (men of learning), all Arabic terms are listed in their singular form only, with plurals formed by the addition of s.

Sūsī, Mukhtār as- (cont.)
mān, 111-12; al-Ma'sūl, 42,
88n, 122, 149, 162n; reformist
lectures in Marrakesh, 93, 94,
97, 115

Tabbā', 'Abd al-'Azīz at- (shrine),
79, 86, 93
tafsīr (Quranic exegesis), 64
ṭālibs (students): leadership among,
79, 83-84; rural-urban distinc-
tions, 9-10, 60-61, 76-78; ties
with teachers, 79-80, 82-85, 88,
95. See also fqīh; 'ilm; education, Islamic; madrasas; mosque
universities
ṭarīqas (religious orders), 48; attitudes toward, in 1930s, 114-22,
131-32; and colonial administration, 148. See also Darqāwa; al-
Kittānī, Shaykh 'Abd al-Ḥayy;
Kittāniya; Tijāniya
tarjama (autobiography and biography), 29; of 'Abd ar-Raḥmān,
55-56, 107; colonial ties in, 138;
history in, 42; representation of
self in, 41-42, 53-56
Tijāniya (religious order), 116
Touarti, 'Alī bin al-Mu'allim at-,
162n

'ulamā' (men of learning), 3-4, 6,

8; and colonial rule, 6-7, 164-65;
marriages of, 46-47; in politics,
7, 115, 152-53, 165-66, 177-80;
rhetorical style of, 87-88; as social category, 9, 104-106, 121-
22; social responsibility of, 104,
130-34, 160, 166; and sulṭa,
133; visiting Bzu, 121-22
understanding, in religious studies,
see under education, Islamic
'Uthmān, Muḥammad ibn (d.
1944), 115, 162

women: in court, 117-18; domestic
authority of, 51-53; education
of, 61, 172; social roles of, 26,
34-35, 47, 123
writing: notarial, 26-27; styles of,
29; uses of, 60

Yūsī, Sīdī al-Ḥasan al- (1631-
1691), 14, 52
Yūsufiya, 4-5, 85-106, 161; French
intervention in, 162; as institution, 86; rectors of, 162-63, 171;
ruralization of, in 1930s, 163-64;
as student hostel, 80-81. See also
mosque universities

zāwiyas (religious lodges), as centers of learning, 54n, 68, 113

LIBRARY OF CONGRESS CATALOGING IN PUBLICATION DATA

Eickelman, Dale F., 1942–
Knowledge and power in Morocco.

Bibliography: p.
Includes index.
1. Islam—Education—Morocco.   2. Mansuri,
'Abd ar-Rahman.   3. Muslims—Morocco—Biography.
4. Morocco—Intellectual life.   I. Title
LC911.M65E38   1985   370'.964   85-3444
ISBN 0-691-09415-2